CRAZY DIDN'T GET ME

Preparation for My Destiny

Cynthia Mobley Howell

HOWELL ARE YOU PUBLISHING COMPANY

ISBN: 978-1-960001-02-3 (Paperback)
ISBN: 978-1-960001-03-0 (eBook)
Library of Congress Control Number: 202292218

Editor: Melanie James
Cover Design: Juan Roberts, Creative Lunacy
Literary Director: Sandra Slayton James

Published by:

Howell Are You Publishing Company |
www.cynthiamobleyhowell.com

Printed in the United States of America

DEDICATION

Crazy Didn't Get Me: Preparation for My Destiny is dedicated to my three brothers, James, Billy, and Dwight, who are my inspiration for writing this book and lending my voice to advocate for the Mental Health Community.

FOREWORD

Crazy Didn't Get Me: Preparation for My Destiny
Foreword
Dr. Shawn Fair

"Mental health . . . is not a destination, but a process. It's about how you drive, not where you're going."

—Noah Shpancer, Ph.D

If "I don't look like what I've been through" was a person, it would be Cynthia Mobley Howell. While this statement may appear like an often heard "cliché," it is nonetheless true. While we may all marvel at her million-dollar smile, flawless skin, and figure that would make a supermodel jealous, Cynthia spent years hiding the pain of secrets and shame of growing up in a household of mental illness. Through her unwavering commitment to healing from past traumas and fueled by a strong sense of faith and courage, she is breaking her silence and using her voice to help heal, empower, and transform others.

As the founder of the Leadership Experience Tour, the #1 platform for speakers in the United States, we provide an opportunity for new and emerging speakers to share their message with the world. Cynthia was carefully vetted and chosen in April 2021 to speak at the event. My selection team knew within 30 seconds of hearing her presentation that she was a gifted presenter. Her message on mental health advocacy was dynamically delivered, engaging, motivating, inspirational, and transformational. Cynthia has the ability to connect with the audience through content that is relational and, at times, funny, reflective, and emotional. She provided a speaking experience that our audience will talk about for years to come.

Cynthia's influence has evolved to being recognized as one of the leading voices for mental health advocacy. Known for her mantra, "I'm Not Keeping Quiet Anymore," she impacts audiences with her quest to normalize mental health conversations. She trains audiences worldwide to eradicate mental health stigmas and adopt compassion, awareness, and acceptance. She advocates for a world where we can break the silence and encourage early intervention. Cynthia now utilizes the same masterful skills she possesses to win listeners through her skillful speaking on stage and win readers through her gifted writing in her latest book.

In Crazy Didn't Get Me: Preparation for My Destiny, author Cynthia Mobley Howell vividly shares the details of her experiences growing up in a family where all three of her siblings battled with mental illness. Her experience echoes that of countless other families who have come forward with their stories about the challenges of growing up with loved ones who are mentally ill and who have been forced to overcome numerous additional stigma-related obstacles that cause them to struggle in silence.

Within these pages lies the shocking and transparent story of one woman brave enough to share her journey and bold enough to share the challenges she faced along the way. Her powerful testimony of responding to hallucinations, delusions, violence, and anger; helping her loved ones comply with treatment plans and medication; navigating the often-convoluted mental health system; dealing with mental health professionals; and managing stress, all while trying not to lose her own sanity.

Imagine growing up, living, and surviving in a household with three severely mentally ill brothers where schizophrenic outbursts, manic rage, and violent behavior were part of a typical daily routine. Written with compassion and kindness, this book is essential reading for individuals and families seeking expert guidance on diagnosis, treatment, and recovery, featuring an inspiring true story from a resilient woman in her own words. Families and friends are often left in the dark about how best to help their loved ones, deal with logistical issues, and manage the emotional challenges of loving someone suffering. This book is designed to guide family and friends of people with mental illness on understanding their reactions and feelings, how to avoid the damage they can cause, and how to help their loved ones.

The pandemic and other challenges of the last few years have made it apparent to everyone the importance of mental health and the availability of mental health resources. This book addresses how to survive in an environment of mental illness, recognize critical signs of the onset of a mental health issue, and act promptly to seek professional help. Studies show that one in five adults in the United States lives with a mental illness, and millions of people are affected yearly. Everyone affected by a mental illness deserves to live an ordinary, productive, fulfilling life. Early intervention is the key.

Dr. Shawn Fair
Global Keynote Speaker | Leadership Trainer | Consultant | CEO, Fair Consulting Group | Founder, Leadership Experience Tour

CONTENTS

INTRODUCTION

Once I took the plunge and BLASTED myself on a Facebook Live platform that I was writing my first book; I knew that there was no turning back! The response from my followers was surprising and overwhelming to say the least. The countless comments that were often laced with loads of encouragement and support repeatedly left me in an emotional state. I would later sit and bawl my eyes out, for moments at a time. I would then hop on my laptop and start typing because I now knew that a myriad of people were waiting to hear my story.

After surviving growing up in a household filled with intense drama on a regular basis due to sibling mental illness; I started saying that I was going to draft a book one day. I wanted the world to hear my story. Now let me just clarify that it wasn't always a house of horrors. Somewhere along the line, things took a turn for the worse and I felt as though I had landed smack dab inside the walls of an insane asylum.

When I would share with others that I was going to write a book, I was thinking that I would just tell my story. When I finally decided to pen the book, I realized that it was not just simply about "telling my story," but it was about educating and giving hope.

My hope and prayer was that I would become a resonant voice to let others know that mental illness is REAL and it's no joke. I believe that as a result of reading my story that others would recognize that they are not alone, and they don't have to keep quiet about mental illness. Unfortunately, my family paid a supreme price for staying silent.

Even as I was drafting this book, I encountered many people who confirmed to me that my story needed to be told. I had assumed that the stigma of suffering from mental illness was a thing of the past, however; it didn't take me very long to realize this was far from the truth. When I would share with others that I was writing a book and told them what it was about; I was amazed at some of the responses. One such response was from a young lady. When I told her what my book was about, she felt safe enough to share with me that she was suffering from a particular mental illness and how it was affecting her life.

Mental illness is not something that's always easily detectable. An individual can appear to be "perfectly normal," but could be suffering from a mental illness. This is primarily one reason that it was vitally important for me to write this book. There are still too many people that are, *in the closet.* Those who suffer from a mental illness, or who have a family member that's affected by a mental illness should not be afraid of being judged or looked down on about a condition that is beyond their control.

It's amazing how the vast majority of people are inclined to view mental illness much differently from any other type of disease.

A physical disease is of the body and requires treatment, and a mental illness is of the mind and necessitates treatment as well. It's nothing to be ashamed about.

I was ecstatic upon receiving the revelation of what the title of my book should be. I thought the title was catchy and captured exactly what I would write. Then one day I began to second guess myself about the title. My apprehension was that the title would be offensive to some because of the use of that word, "*crazy.*" There's something about using the word, *crazy,* to describe someone with a mental health issue that makes folk a bit uneasy. If we're using it in jest, that's one thing, but to use it in reference to a certified mental illness is another thing. I suppose, mentally ill, would be more politically correct.

I must say, if you're offended by my book title, I apologize to you in advance, but this is the title that GOD GAVE ME, and I MUST be obedient to HIM!

So, my prayer is that as you read *Crazy Didn't Get Me: Preparation for My Destiny*, that you will feel my pain of having to watch, not one, not two, but ALL of my siblings be ravaged by the effects of mental health issues. I hope that I can provide you with some insight and education, and that I can offer hope to those indirectly affected.

I'm sure that if those of us involved could turn back the hands of time, and we knew then what we know now, things would have turned out differently for my siblings.

CHAPTER 1

RUN FOR YOUR LIFE!

I was abruptly awakened from a nap about mid-afternoon that day to the sound of Mama's frightened voice desperately pleading, "James, don't hit me with that board." Still a little groggy from my nap, I rolled out of bed and stumbled out of my bedroom, which was right next to Mama's, and into her bedroom to find Mama and James in a face off. She was standing there in sheer terror in her very petite, five-foot-two-inch, one hundred and ten pound frame.

Mama was standing about fifteen to twenty feet away from James, entirely empty-handed, and it was very clear by the strained look on her face, and the panic in her voice that she was extremely rattled by the whole situation that was taking place. James, on the other hand, was slightly over six feet tall and weighed in at about one-hundred and eighty pounds, with a solid build. On top of the fact that he was already nearly twice Mama's size, he happened to be holding a two-by-four board in his hand. He had it raised and positioned in a manner that suggested that he was about to strike Mama. It didn't take rocket science to know that the odds were definitely stacked against Mama, and it was pretty obvious as to which one of them was going to win this one.

As soon as I entered the room, James immediately took his attention off of Mama and all eyes were on me. I instantly knew that Mama was no longer his intended target and mentally prepared myself for what was about to take place.

When James' and my eyes met, the look in his eyes was a look I pray I never see again in my lifetime. The look on James' face, at that moment, brought real meaning to the term "madman." In an instant, everything erupted into a tailspin. With lightning bolt and jackal speed, James dashed towards me swinging the two-by-four board, and before I could get out of his way, the blow that was originally intended for Mama landed squarely on my left shoulder. I couldn't believe that he had hit me with that board.

Stunned by his actions, and at the same time needing to lash out at the one who had hurt me so badly, I stumbled backwards out of the room, angry, and with revenge on my mind.

My anger superseded the pain I was feeling in my shoulder. That's when I spotted one of Mama's favorite clay flowerpots. By that time, James had come out of Mama's bedroom and was standing in our dining room. I grabbed that clay flowerpot and with all of the strength that I could muster, I flung that pot towards James hoping and praying that it would land smack-dab in his face.

My intent was to make him feel pain like I was feeling. But instead of the flowerpot landing in James's face, it missed him altogether and went crashing straight through the glass portion of Mama's beautiful China cabinet that she was working so hard to pay for.

My failed attempt to retaliate infuriated this already mad man and he swiftly started moving towards me. As he started coming towards me, there was no doubt in my mind that if he got his hands on me in that moment, I would become minced meat. It was crucial for me to get to the front door and out of it before James could reach me, otherwise, I would be history.

With the front door to my back and James facing me, I quickly spun around and started running towards the front door. I'll have to admit that up to this point in life, running had always been a challenge for me. I couldn't even make it around the track in middle school without running out of breath. But isn't it amazing that when you're in a desperate situation, things that seemed hard or even impossible before, all of a sudden become doable? That day, I gave new meaning to the words dash and sprint.

I chuckle now when I think back on that day as I recall how I bolted out of the front door. Oddly, it's a little comical now, but it was not funny at all at the time. I kept telling myself that if I could just make it out of the front door, I'd be okay. Thank God, I did, indeed, make it out the front door before James could grab me.

Once I was outside, with my heart palpitating and adrenaline flowing, I didn't look back and I didn't stop running. Once I did finally look back, it didn't take me long to realize that this ordeal was far from over because James was in hot pursuit of me. He had stride on his side because of his long legs, but fear and youth were in my favor. I am thoroughly convinced that those two things were instrumental in keeping me alive or from suffering great bodily harm that day. The fear of what would happen to me if James had gotten his hands on me caused me to become as light as a feather on my feet. And the fact that I was significantly younger than him gave me the endurance that I needed to outrun him. I say it was those two things; fear, and youth, that saved me.

I put the glory where it really belongs; it was nothing but the grace of God that preserved me that day. The chase seemed like it lasted forever, but in reality, it was only for a few moments.

Another glance back revealed that James was losing steam and I knew that it wouldn't be long before the chase would be over. Just when I felt as though my lungs would explode from all of the hard running, I looked back once again and saw James falling to the ground.

Fortunately for me, I was able to outrun James who had chased me until he literally collapsed from exhaustion, right in the middle of our street. It was then, and only then, that I was sure I was no longer in danger. I stopped running, and after catching my breath, I could relax, knowing that James was no longer a threat to me, at least in that moment.

By that time, law enforcement and paramedics had been called to the scene. After the paramedics made sure that he was okay, James was placed in the ambulance and taken to the local hospital and admitted to the Mental Health Unit. I hobbled back to the house, still a little weak in the knees and went inside and knocked out on the sofa. Thank God there would be peace in the household now, at least for 72 hours. That's how long James would stay in the Mental Health Unit to become stabilized. James, my oldest brother had been suffering for quite some time from bipolar disorder.

> **Bipolar Disorder** - *a chronic mood disorder that causes intense shifts in mood, energy levels and behavior. Manic and hypomanic episodes are the main sign of the condition, and most people with bipolar disorder also have depressive episodes. The condition is manageable with medications, talk therapy, lifestyle changes and other treatments. (Cleveland Clinic)*

> **Fact** - *46 million people around the world, including 2.8% of the U.S. population, have bipolar disorder. (SingleCare)*

CHAPTER 2

CHURCH WAS NOT A CHOICE

My three older brothers and I grew up in an extremely strict household having been raised by parents who were very devout Christians. Being devout is one thing, but my Mama was extreme.

Her gross misinterpretation of some portions of the Bible caused her to impose a ridiculous list of dos and don'ts, mostly don'ts. These restrictions cramped our lifestyle as children. Now mind you, there was some validity to some of the rules and regulations that were handed down to us that she claims were based on God's Word, but some of her notions were utterly unfounded and just plain asinine. I concluded that her lack of enlightenment would be a direct indication of how things would eventually shake out in the lives of me and my brothers. My brothers and I, along with our parents, would spend endless hours at church, week in and week out. You might say that we, meaning the children, overdosed on church. I know I'd had my belly full of it.

Our church schedule started on Sunday morning when we would have to rise and shine early to get dressed in our Sunday best to get to Sunday school by ten o'clock. Sunday school lasted a grueling hour or so. Yes, it was grueling. Then following Sunday school, we would enter into what was called morning service. Morning service usually began around eleven thirty, and depending on how things went, it could last until two o'clock or even later into the afternoon. I don't recall us having breakfast at home before we left for church in the morning. So, on top of the long hours at church, our bellies were empty.

We would return home after morning service for a few hours and then have to head out again to be back at the church by five o'clock, for what was called YPCW (Young People Christian Workers). This would last for approximately two hours or so, and then we would enter into what was called night service. Night service usually began around seven or eight o'clock and could very easily last until past ten o'clock at night. I remember many times getting so sleepy that I would have to lie down on one of the pews and go to sleep.

It wasn't enough that we spent such long hours in church, but we could never seem to go right home after it was over. My parents, mostly Mama, would linger and talk to the other church folks for what seemed like hours. Finally, when I thought I would bust wide open from boredom and sleepiness, we would finally head home.

There were no church services on Monday or Tuesday, so we got a little break. I'm sure something else must have been going on at the church at least one of those days, but thank God, we weren't required to attend. When Wednesday rolled around, we were right back at it again. This time for prayer and Bible study. I don't think the big deal was the fact that we had to be there once again on Wednesday because it wasn't unusual for most churches to have a mid-week service.

However, the issue for us, as children, was the endless hours that were spent once we got there, at least the hours seemed endless to me.

Nowadays, if it even looks like a church service is going past an hour and a half, folks start getting antsy. Let me just say, they wouldn't have been able to hang with us back in the day. Thank God, we would get another break from church on Thursdays, but we'd be right back at it again on Fridays.

I think of all the services that we attended during the week; Friday had to be the worst. Friday service was called tarry service, or for the young folks, we probably would rather have referred to it as "torture" service. I don't know what bright mind came up with this concept of a tarry service, but it was one of the most ludicrous things I had ever heard of! You see, someone had come up with this whacky idea that in order to receive Christ into your heart as your personal Savior, that you had to get down on your knees in front of the altar and literally repeat the name 'Jesus' over and over again, so He could "come into your heart."

Supposedly, how one would recognize that Jesus had come into your heart was that some type of feeling would come over you that would make your body jerk and quake, you would begin speaking in another language, or maybe even foam at the mouth. At that point, you would be released to get up from the altar, and you were now considered "saved."

When I became much older and looked back on this whole church thing, some of what happened was quite amusing, to say the least. Oh, I could tell you some stories. Anyway, I just wanted to give you a snapshot of the whole church scenario as it related to our upbringing.

Now with that in mind, the sad part about all of this was that it didn't leave room for much recreation for us because my Mama believed that almost everything was a sin unless it had something to do with "church."

It's no wonder, that at age nineteen when Daddy died; for a time, I ran as far away from church as I could.

I'm mentioning this whole church routine, primarily because it greatly contributed to how my parents would respond later on when my brothers' lives would begin to show signs that something had gone terribly wrong.

Based on my current understanding of what it means to be a Christian, the very thing that should have worked on my brothers' behalf; unfortunately, along with some other factors, ended up working against my brothers.

Mama believed that being a Christian meant that you shouldn't play any type of sports, go to amusement parks, go to the beach, play board games, cards, or for that matter, do anything that was fun; according to Mama, these activities were all sinful. I never understood who or what had influenced her to come to this absurd conclusion, but this was her story, and she was sticking to it.

All of the other neighborhood kids were making their mark in school playing; football, basketball, running track, and doing all the things that kids do, but my brothers and I were not allowed. I recall my oldest brother being in the band in his middle school years. I don't know how he got that one past Mama.

When our neighbors would load up their families to enjoy some fun and sun at the beach, we had to watch as they drove past, all the while longing for the same experience. If we were lucky, we were asked to join them, but that was seldom the case.

Now you would've thought that was bad enough, but it didn't stop there. It gets worse. You probably are wondering how it could get any worse. Well, it did.

I am fairly confident when I say that we were the only family in the city, (perhaps the state), that didn't own a television. Yes, you've probably already guessed it. We didn't own a television because according to Mama, this was a sin as well. The cardinal sin. I have often wondered what American household in the twentieth century didn't own a television (by choice)?

I remember how Mama always equated watching a television to watching a movie at a theatre. In her mind, going to the movie theatre, or as she called it, the "pictcha" show, would buy you a one-way ticket to hell. She said that having a television in the house was just like going to the "pitcha" show, and she wasn't having it.

Since almost everything but going to church was a sin, what was a child to do for recreation? It's incredible to think that Mama wondered why I was such a rebellious child.

On a good note, however, I suppose I have my Mama to thank for my love of reading books, since I could barely do anything else. So pretty much, my spare time was spent reading, reading, and then reading some more.

My brother Dwight, not to be outdone about my family not owning a television, was almost a permanent fixture at our next-door neighbor's home. He was determined that he would not be deprived of watching television. He spent most of his afternoons and evenings invading our neighbor's home, perched in front of their television set. I'm not exactly sure what my other two brothers did to entertain themselves, but I'm sure that behind Mama's back, they were doing some of the exact things that she had forbidden.

Finally, at age thirteen, when it almost no longer mattered to me; for the first time in our lives, we had a television in the home. This was shocking. Let me clarify that it was not Daddy, nor was it Mama who bought the television.

My brother Donny became old enough to get a job. Little did any of us know that all along, in the back of his mind, he had plans to purchase a television for our home. At his first opportunity, without asking for permission; he just bought it and planted it squarely in our living room.

We were all shaking in our boots and holding our breath considering his bold and defiant move. Knowing how Mama felt about having a television in the house, he could not possibly have been thinking clearly. I don't know how he managed to pull this off, but he did.

For reasons unknown, Mama; much to everyone's surprise, didn't make a big fuss about the television. You might be wondering why Mama had the "say-so" about having a television and why Daddy never ran interference.

Daddy could not have cared less one way or the other. He never bothered about the matter of the television because he was immersed in what clearly mattered to him and brought him pleasure; his precious automobiles. Never mind his children being able to enjoy some of the pleasures of their choice. As long as he had a fine car, all was well in the world. He most often went along with whatever Mama said or did. Daddy definitely was not henpecked; rather, he was just passive.

The television got to stay in the house. The funny thing about it is that after all of those years of us not having a television because of Mama's staunch religious beliefs; she must have re-evaluated her convictions. She actually began watching television herself at some point. I guess she realized that having a television wasn't a one-way ticket to hell and not so bad after all, and furthermore, she was outnumbered.

My Mama grew up in a family of talented singers. That beautiful talent was passed down to me and my brothers. We all sang in church, especially my brothers. The three of them formed a singing group and were known as "The Mobley Brothers." Although they were still in their adolescent years when they sang together, they were a force to be reckoned with. I recall hearing in later years that they were admired, but at the same time often envied in the church circle. Admired, because they were great singers, and envied for the same reason.

Back in those days whenever there was any type of church convention; Friday night was designated as "Youth Night." During "Youth Night," there was always a talent show that consisted primarily of singing, and a 1st, 2nd, and 3rd place prize for the winners. My brothers would usually participate in the talent shows and the story is told that The Mobley Brothers always walked away with the 1st place prize, and for some folks this was a major issue.

My brothers continued to sing together into their late teens. Then they reached the age where Daddy and Mama could really no longer force them to go to church. My two oldest brothers, James, and Donny ended up falling by the wayside, but my youngest brother, Dwight, kept on going to church. He landed a position as pianist for the youth choir. I think the only thing that kept him going as long as he did was that it was a paid position.

Dwight was rolling right along until some of the older church folks started complaining about his long hair. The belief among these older church folks was that it was a sin for men to wear their hair long. They tried to force Dwight to cut his hair, but he wasn't having it. There was bickering back and forth about this for quite some time, and neither Dwight nor the church folks was willing to give in. He refused to cut his hair and they refused to stop harassing him about it. In the end, the church got their way because Dwight finally became exhausted by it all and decided that it just wasn't worth it. He didn't cut his hair though. At first, he quit as the pianist for the choir, and eventually he stopped going to church altogether.

At that point, I was not of age to decide whether I would attend church or not, so I was still in attendance. All of my brothers made the decision to stop going to church. I became the last sibling standing as far as church was concerned. Little did any of us know at the time that life would deal our family some serious blows and I would end up being the last sibling standing, literally!

> *Forcing religion may seem like a good idea to some parents. In a way, forcing religion can be seen as a helpful tool to kids, since they think their child will eventually find their faith and believe in what the parents do.*

> *However, this is not the case. You cannot force someone to believe in something. Sure, they might tell you exactly what you want to hear, but what good does that do? A child will always believe what they want to believe, no matter how much those beliefs are forced.* (Global Comment)

CHAPTER 3

WHO ARE THE MOBLEY'S?

From the time I was old enough to remember, Daddy had hair that was as white as snow, and as soft as cotton. It was definitely one of his best features. As I recall, nearly everywhere we went, folks complimented him on his beautiful silver crown.

As a little girl, I never really made a connection between Daddy's white hair and how old he might have been. I didn't make the connection between Daddy's hair and his age until my teenage years. It was then that it occurred to me that Daddy must have been old. That didn't matter to me at all because he was my Daddy and I loved him more than anyone could possibly imagine. Now grey hair is not always necessarily an indication that a person has been around for a very long time, but for Daddy, that was precisely the case.

As a matter of fact, Daddy had been around so long that he didn't know his actual age. Daddy was born during a time when many families didn't record birth dates using birth certificates. Such important events would often times be documented in a family Bible. If that Bible somehow happened to become misplaced, then that information would no longer be available.

In Daddy's case, either his date of birth was never recorded, or the document had been misplaced. I never knew what Daddy's story was regarding his birthdate, I just know that he didn't know when he was born.

Since Daddy didn't seem to have any record of his actual date of birth, he decided that he would just fabricate a birthdate. He decided to use two of my older brothers' birthdates. Why he chose two and not one, I'll never know.

Daddy went from having no birthdate to two birthdates. He chose August 30th and July 15th as his birthdates. When he was asked for his date of birth, whichever of those dates that first popped into his head, was the one that he used. There was still just one issue. He didn't know the year he was born. So, he just picked the age he wanted to be and went from there.

When I was old enough to have some clue as to what was going on and heard him state his age for the first time, he said that he was sixty-six. Incidentally, Daddy remained at age sixty-six for quite a few years. I can vividly recall hearing Mama ask him one day, "How long are you going to be sixty-six?"

Daddy did eventually move his age along, because by the time he passed away, he had finally made it to age seventy-three. Now that's where things became even more interesting with this whole age mystery of my Daddy.

When Daddy passed away, he had an older aunt who was still alive. Her name was Florida Bell; she was known as, Aunt Grown. According to Aunt Grown, Daddy, at the time of his passing would have been in his mid-nineties. She came to that conclusion, based on her recollection that Daddy carried Oree, a friend of the family, on his back when he was a teenager. Oree, she said was much younger than Daddy. Now when Daddy died, Oree, who was still living, was in her late seventies. Aunt Grown concluded that Daddy had been much older than Oree. Based on Aunt Grown's calculations, Daddy was in his nineties. My family concluded based on Daddy's fake age that he would have been around fifty-five at the time of my birth. According to the new information received from Aunt Grown about his calculated actual age, Daddy would have really been in his seventies when I was born. It was during one of our Sunday afternoons drives that I remember Daddy reminiscing about his past.

That particular day, I guess he just felt like talking about some things and so he started telling me about where he was born as well as who his parents were. Daddy said that he had been born in a very small town in Alabama called Hartford. Up until that Sunday afternoon, I had not known much about where Daddy had come from, geographically, or genetically speaking. Daddy told me that his Mama's name was Leila and his Daddy's name was Pete.

That's all I can remember him saying about my paternal grandparents. They passed away long before I was born, so I never got to know them. I never even saw a picture of them. In that same conversation, Daddy also told me that he had some sisters, but I don't remember him ever telling me their names or how many there were. They too had died long before I was born. I recall Daddy saying to me many times that I was built like his sisters. He said that his sisters were very pretty, and I had hips like them.

Daddy also had two brothers: Peter, (Uncle Pete) and Espelee, or (Lee). They were both still living when I was born, and I do remember them. Daddy and his brothers all bore a striking resemblance to one another. Uncle Pete lived in a small town called DeFuniak Springs, Florida, which was about an hour from where we lived, and he would come to visit occasionally. As for Uncle Lee, unfortunately, he had been in the Florida State Hospital, a mental institution, for the past thirty years at that time.

He had been institutionalized for such a long time; neither I nor my siblings had ever gotten to know him. After being institutionalized for some thirty years, Ms. Ella Baker, who was a long-time friend to Daddy and his brothers, somehow sprung Lee from the mental hospital, and he lived with her until he passed away.

As far as his personality, Daddy was a very outgoing man who was always smiling. He had a laugh that usually ended in a snicker, a laugh that Mama totally detested. And I detested her for detesting the laughter of my hero.

Daddy was one of the most kind-hearted people I have ever known. This is not because he was my Daddy, but because that's just the truth. At his funeral service, it was said that his kindness was such that it was as though he carried a little jar of honey around with him, and to everyone that he came in contact with, he would give them just a little pinch of that honey. My Daddy was mostly even tempered and very mild mannered, but there were a few incidents with Daddy that involved my brothers where his behavior proved to be otherwise. I'll tell you about that later.

My Mama was born Florence Ruby Pittman on August 19th, 1923, in Barbour County Alabama. She was the second oldest of seven girls. She didn't have any brothers. I guess all Roosevelt and Annie Mae Pittman could produce were girls. I never knew my granddaddy, Roosevelt, because he died before I was born. He was quite young when he died, only forty-nine.

I did have the awesome pleasure of knowing my grandmamma, who we affectionately called Mama Annie. Mama Annie was as sweet as pie, and I loved it when she visited us. She lived with my Aunt in Miami, and once or twice a year she would come and stay with us for two to three weeks at a time. I must say that those were some of the happiest times at our house. The house would be filled with so much laughter during her visits because Mama Annie was a very happy-go-lucky person. I can still see her skipping through the house while singing her favorite hymn, "At the cross, at the cross where I first saw the light."

The highlight of my evenings was when I brushed Mama Annie's hair before she went to bed at night. She had very long and beautiful hair. I would always have to brush it one hundred strokes because Mama Annie said this made your hair shine. Not only would our house be filled with laughter when Mama Annie came, but it would be filled with lots of good food that we didn't normally eat.

Mama Annie made the best golden crispy fried chicken, that she always drained on a brown paper bag to absorb the grease. Her home-made biscuits were out of this world. They were light and fluffy, and they would melt like butter in your mouth. The highlight of her cooking, for me anyway, was when she would make us that special treat called blueberry doobie that would make you want to slap your mama.

Mama Annie had nicknames for me and my three brothers. She called me TinTin, and she called my oldest brother James, Jamie. I don't remember what Donny's nickname was. Dwight's nickname was Dwightie. When we would find out that Mama Annie was coming to town, we were beside ourselves with excitement and could hardly wait for her to get there. As excited as we were about her coming, we were equally saddened when it was time for her to leave.

Oh, how we loved Mama Annie. Unlike the limited knowledge and contact with Daddy's brothers and sisters, we knew all of our Mama's sisters. The only one that I never knew was Aunt Marie, who died when I was eight years old. So, there was Aunt Julia, Aunt Jewel, Aunt Ellen, Aunt Evelyn, and Aunt Mary. Mama always referred to her and her siblings as "The Seven Sisters."

When Mama would speak about her childhood, I got the feeling that she had considered herself to be a "Miss Goodie Two-Shoes," because to let her tell it, she never did too much of anything wrong. That's what she believed about herself and what she wanted everyone else to believe about her.

Mama became a devout Christian at a young age and going to church was her life. She once told me that she had never smoked a cigarette or taken a drink of liquor in her life. I suppose she must have thought that made her some type of saint. I'll have to admit that Mama did have some very high morals. Likewise, she had her share of shortcomings. I didn't find out about some of her alleged mischievous ways, when she was much younger, until after she passed away in 2011.

One of my aunts spilled the beans and told me some stuff about Mama that certainly did not depict her as the angel of which she had portrayed herself. Now whether my aunt was telling the truth or not, I don't know. Let's just say that we all have some skeletons in our closets, and sometimes that's exactly where they should remain.

There was one thing that I absolutely admired about my Mama. She was very outspoken, and most of the time didn't have a problem letting folks know how she felt about a particular issue. She rarely bit her tongue and was ready to deal with the consequences whenever she gave her opinion on a matter. But what I didn't like about her is that she was very argumentative, always making it her business to have the last say in a confrontation. Mama almost always believed that she was right every time and about everything.

Another thing that I admired about Mama is that she was a woman of integrity and great character. She didn't want to be a part of anything that smelled like dishonesty. I once remember overhearing her telling one of her friends about a situation where someone was encouraging her to be dishonest in order to qualify for Food Stamps. In the words of Mama, and I quote, "I ain't lying just to get a stamp."

There were three things that Mama was known for in our town. Her melodic singing voice, her fashion consciousness (she was always dressed to the nines), and her love for stiletto heels which she wore well into her seventies.

In the late 1940's, when she was in her mid-twenties, Mama moved from Alabama to Panama City, Florida where she met Daddy. They ended up getting married and started a family. All of this took place within a span of about three years because my oldest brother was born on August 30th, 1951. They named him James Oliver. I remember James being mostly quiet and rather introverted. In school, he wasn't the brightest star in the sky, I remember him having to be in Special Education classes. Even though James was somewhat of an introvert, he still had lots of friends. I never knew where he got it, but his nickname was "Blee." Now the only person that called him that was his buddies. Our family always called him James.

James was the lone ranger for almost two years and then Billy Don came along on July 15th, 1953. Among close friends and family he was known as Donny, everyone else knew him as Billy. I would often find myself explaining to folks that Billy and Donny were one and the same person. Donny was the ladies' man. He was as cool as a cucumber and as smooth as silk. He was known for how he glided and strided when he walked. Back then they called it "pimping" or "dapping."

Well Mama and Daddy waited only one year to have the next child who came on October 25th, 1954. This third bundle of joy was named Dwight Earl. It's funny because the very first thing that comes to mind when I mention Dwight is his name. That's because none of us siblings could correctly pronounce his name. Now that's kind of strange because Mama and Daddy, other relatives, and friends pronounced his name correctly. James, Donny, and I were the only ones that called him "Gwight." Dwight had a very outgoing and fiery personality. He was fun to be around and full of energy. I can picture him now doing back flips from the beginning to the end of the dirt road that we lived on. He was very limber.

Dwight loved displaying his gymnastic abilities in front of all of the neighborhood children. He was the one that believed in calling his own shots. He pretty much did what he wanted to do and if anyone dared to challenge him, they would be in for a fight. That fight could have been verbal or physical. He didn't pick fights, but if he was ever provoked into a fight, that person would very soon be awfully sorry. I don't recall him ever losing a fight. Everyone eventually learned not to be deceived by the fact that he was as thin as a rail. If he ever got loose on you, he could do some real damage. He often didn't fight fair for the simple reason that his opponents were typically much bigger than him. When you encountered him in a fight, you got him along with whatever aids he chose to use. He didn't mess around. He wasn't taking a chance on losing.

My commentary on Dwight is obviously lengthier than that of my other two brothers because he would prove to be the most dramatic of the three.

Five years after Dwight, on October 6, 1959, the long-awaited rose of the garden came on the scene. That would be none other than yours truly, Cynthia Marzetta. My parents had been hoping and praying for a girl for the longest time. They got their girl but being around all those boys turned me into a bona fide tomboy.

I remember Mama dressing me in little frilly dresses for school and sending me off looking like a little princess, but by the time I returned home from school, I looked like I'd been in a fight with a grizzly bear. The little frilly dresses were usually hanging off of me. I had a habit of stopping by the big tree that was in the empty field across from our house, just before I got home. I'd climb it until the branches had ripped my dress to shreds. My Mama would *whup my behind* every time but I would just do it all over again the next day. I was suffering from the "can't-help-its." But the fact of the matter is, I didn't wanna help it. I was just not the little girlie girl that Mama wanted me to be.

I was surrounded by all of that testosterone, and it was rubbing off on me in a serious way.

So, there you have us—the Mobley family.

> **Family**—*The basic unit in society traditionally consisting of two parents rearing their children.* (Merriam-Webster)

CHAPTER 4

NOT THE IDEAL FAMILY

Our family, like most families, had its fair share of dysfunction. But normal dysfunction coupled with half of us suffering from mental illness turned into what I dubbed "*The Nightmare On 9th Court*."

My experience became for me The Nightmare on 9th Court because of the many nightmarish episodes that I lived through in that house. A nightmare is full of torment and horror, misery, and agony, and I felt all of that and more at house number 1002. I would be lying if I told you that all of my encounters at home were less than joyous. There must have been times when I was able to wear a smile, but as I allow my mind to walk down memory lane, it just seems like the bad times outweighed the good times.

Maybe being the avid reader that I was, I had run across too many books where families were depicted totally differently from what I was experiencing. In most of the books I read, everyone woke up in the morning from a peaceful night's rest and the kids hear Daddy and Mommy greeting each other with a loving "*Good Morning*" as they shared an affectionate kiss. Then Mommy goes into the kid's rooms and gives them an endearing good morning, prodding them to get up, get dressed and prepare for breakfast that would soon be ready.

The family would gather at the breakfast table, and everyone bows as Daddy offers a prayer to bless the food and their day. They keep the conversation pretty light as everyone chimes in about the expectations of their day. They finish eating breakfast, the kitchen is cleaned, and everyone is off to the races. Later, they all return home after a day of work and school.

Mommy helps the kids with their homework while cooking dinner, and the family once again meets around the table. The family shares a great dinner as they talk about the events of their day. After dinner, they hang out together for a little while, perhaps enjoying games and laughter.

Everyone eventually grabs their favorite spot to relax and after a while, off to bed they all go. They not only enjoy these pleasurable times with family, but at different intervals throughout the course of the year, the family takes fun vacations and enjoy each other's company. This becomes a time for much-needed rest and relaxation.

Of course, what I know now that I didn't know then is everything that I was reading in those books wasn't necessarily a reality in many families. It certainly wasn't in mine. Things went on in families contrary to what the books depicted. The only thing is that from outside appearances, it seemed as though no other family on our street was dealing with the type of turbulence that our family was regularly entertaining.

Yes, you would occasionally hear of a situation where a family may have been having problems with one child or another that may have been having some issues, but it would be pretty mild in comparison to our drama that was usually completely out of the box and off the charts!

Most people could not even begin to imagine what it would be like to live in a house where literally half of the family is disturbed.

Consider these qualities when evaluating how well your own family is functioning:

- Is there ample humor and fun within your family, despite the very real demands of daily life?
- Does your family have rules that have been clearly stated and are evenly applied, yet are flexible and respond to new situations and changes in the family?
- Are the family's expectations of each person reasonable, realistic, mutually agreed upon and generally fulfilled?
- Do family members have the support to achieve most of their individual goals, and are their personal needs being met?
- Do parents and children have genuine respect for one another, demonstrating love, caring trust, and concern, even when there are disagreements?
- Is your family able to mature and change without everyone getting upset or unhappy? (healthychildren.org)

CHAPTER 5

HE WENT OVERBOARD

Earlier I shared that Daddy was a rather mild-mannered man, but had done a few things that showed a side that was less than mild mannered. One of those things that comes to mind is the evening that Daddy—the church Deacon, violently pounded Dwight's head into the fireplace hearth. Ironically, the very thing that was designed to provide warmth and comfort became quite the opposite on that particular evening. We were relatively poor and unfortunately, the only house that we could afford was an older frame house that we were renting. The house did not have an adequate heating system and our means of heating was a lone fireplace in the living room and space heaters that were spread throughout the eight-room house.

Most times, we would all hang out in the living room to be near the fireplace to try and stay warm until time for bed. The space heaters were strategically placed throughout the house. Occasionally, we would wander off to another room before turning in for the night, but most of the time we would quickly return to the living room because the other rooms were just too cold. Truthfully, it wasn't that warm in the living room. We were really only warm if we either stood directly in front of or pulled a chair right up to the fireplace. The only problem with that was, the front of our bodies would usually get too hot, while meanwhile our backside would still be cold. It was pretty much a no-win situation.

For the fireplace, we used kindling wood to keep the fire burning. The fire was initially lit by pouring kerosene on the wood and then we would roll up several old newspaper pages and light them from the kitchen stove then place them underneath the wood to get the blaze going. After a while the fire would start to dwindle and to keep it going, we had to add more wood and or kerosene. Everyone but me would take turns with this process. For some reason, the only one who had issues with this task was Dwight.

The issue was that when Dwight would try to pour the kerosene into the fireplace on the wood, he would always manage to spill a good portion of it on the hearth which would cause the fire to flare up and come dangerously close to the carpet.

Time and time again Daddy had warned Dwight to be careful about that because he could start a fire. Despite the fact that Dwight tried his very best to not spill the kerosene on the hearth, he always managed to do so anyway. He just couldn't get it right. One day I overheard Daddy threaten Dwight, and his words blew me away. He told Dwight that the next time he spilled kerosene on the hearth, he was going to make him lick it up. Of course, Daddy really didn't mean that he was gonna make Dwight lick the kerosene up, right? Wrong.

What should have been and could have been a teachable moment that evening turned into child abuse. Yes, I'm calling it what it is. CHILD ABUSE!

Now Daddy was not a mean man at all, but he had his flaws like everyone else. He rarely disciplined us, but on the few occasions when he did, the punishment never seemed to fit the crime. As much as I hate to admit it, Daddy had a ridiculously barbaric method of disciplining. He was definitely lacking in this area of parenting skills. It's been said that, parenting doesn't come with a manual, and that's too bad, because in this case, Daddy needed one badly!

I had no clue about Daddy's upbringing. I only knew his parents' names, and that was about it. I had no idea what his family situation was like; if he was raised by both of his parents or even if his father was present in his life; and if he was, what type of role model had he been. From what I could remember, Daddy told me that he either never attended school or had very little schooling. He claimed that he couldn't read, although I would watch him regularly reading the Bible. Maybe he meant he couldn't read well.

Daddy did "yard work" as he called it to support our family. He was a master at what he did. I remember him being in very high demand because of his excellent skills in landscaping. He never went to school for it, but he knew the names of every plant and flower, and he could manicure a lawn so perfectly that it could easily have qualified for the front cover of *Better Homes and Gardens* magazine.

He worked for some of the wealthiest white folk in our town, but sad to say they never paid him for what he was worth. He often took my brothers along to help him, promising to pay them on Friday but many Fridays came and went with either no payday for them or a partial payday with a promise of the remainder to come, which often never did.

Time and again I would overhear my brothers complaining about not being paid. They would talk about how they had made plans for the weekend and then their plans would be ruined because Daddy hadn't followed through on his promise to pay them. I remember feeling bad for them when they didn't get their money. I would help Daddy out myself sometimes by sweeping the grass off the sidewalks after he had mowed the lawn. But unlike my brothers, payday was never an issue for me. Just being with my Daddy and being treated to McDonalds afterwards was payday enough for me.

Daddy was a kind and gentle man, but he always stood up for himself and called folk out when they were wrong. He always gave my friends money when they were leaving after visiting me. He would say to them, "Here, let me give you a lil piece of money." In my eyesight, my Daddy could do no wrong.

But he did have that somewhat of a dark side to him on occasion. It seemed to only surface though whenever it concerned my brothers.

So that particular evening it was Dwight who was pouring the kerosene on the fire and as usual and unfortunately for him, the kerosene ended up splashing all over the hearth.

Brace yourself as I tell you what happened next. Even to this day, I would like to believe that I imagined this, but my imagination is not that vigorous. This actually happened.

Dwight was pouring the kerosene on the fire, and it was spilling onto the hearth. None of us saw Daddy coming. It was as if he had come out of nowhere, and before anyone could blink, he reached for Dwight and somehow managed to grab him by both of his feet. He flipped him upside down and began pounding his head into the hearth while yelling "lick it up, lick it up, lick it up!"

I was sure that Daddy was going to kill Dwight because the awful thudding sounds that were being heard as Dwight's head was being pounded into the cement was dreadful. I would love to be able to describe to you what injuries to Dwight that Daddy's horrendous actions produced, but I don't remember. I believe I was so traumatized by all of this that I just blocked that part out. All I know is that I couldn't believe what had just taken place. It was nothing but the grace of God that my brother didn't die that night. That was probably the first time that I saw Daddy in such a negative light. I can understand a child suffering in this manner at the hands of a stranger, but to have the one who is supposed to love, nurture, and protect you, put you through this type of ordeal is unthinkable. After watching my brother's head being repeatedly pounded into that stone hearth, it makes sense that Dwight would experience mental health issues later in life.

While writing this portion of the book, my interest really became peaked on the subject of head trauma as it relates to mental illness, so I decided to do just a little research on it. My findings confirmed what I had already suspected. In an article entitled "*Head Trauma May Boost Schizophrenia Risk*" by Rachael Rettner, she wrote, "Mary Cannon, of the Royal College of Surgeons in Dublin, and colleagues analyzed nine previous studies that included participants who had suffered Traumatic Brain Injury (TBI) and participants from the general population that had not suffered TBI. Overall, TBI was associated with an increased risk of schizophrenia. Dr. Dolores Malaspina, a professor of psychiatry and environmental medicine at New York University said, 'Brain injury can pull on and break neural connections, which can have real, biological consequences. Depression and personality changes are common repercussions of TBI. And there are some cases in which a patient has developed schizophrenia due in part to their TBI. Some people may have genes that predispose them to schizophrenia once they experience an environmental "trigger," such as TBI.

Although these facts confirmed what I already believed, it was just a little disturbing to have to consider that my beloved Daddy's awful disciplinary action that night had contributed to my brothers' eventual illness.

The second and only other time that I witnessed Daddy doing something incredibly shocking and appalling to my brothers was when Daddy's silver dollar collection went missing. For some reason when he couldn't find his collection, he automatically assumed that one of my brothers had stolen it. After asking each of them several times if they had taken it and they all insisted they hadn't, Daddy decided that somebody was lying and since he couldn't get them to simply TELL the truth, he was going to BEAT the truth out of them.

Now I don't know which incident was worse. The incident with Daddy pounding Dwight's head into the hearth, or the one I'm about to tell you about.

Go ahead and strap on your seatbelt because you're about to go for a discomforting ride!

Everyone had sort of been deceived into thinking that all was well since Daddy calmly walked away from the situation and outside to his truck after not being able to get a "truthful" answer from my brothers. Little did any of us know what was running through his mind, and if we had known perhaps a cry to God for some serious intervention would have gone up to the heavens.

Daddy eventually came back inside the house and in his hands, he was carrying a couple of the ropes that he used for securing equipment onto his truck bed. Of course, we were all very curious as to what he intended to do with the ropes. Sadly, his plans for those ropes would turn into actions by him that should have landed him underneath the county jail, or maybe even prison for a very long time.

He first instructed my brothers to strip off all of their clothes, and I DO mean ALL of them, including underwear, and surprisingly, they complied.

He then tied their wrists with one of the ropes to the old upright black piano that was in our dining room. I often wondered why my brothers were so compliant with his wishes to strip naked and then be tied to the piano like animals.

Mind you, my brothers were not little kids, but teenagers. It wasn't like they couldn't have resisted. And if push came to shove, the three of them together surely could have very easily overpowered Daddy. Now they would likely afterwards have suffered the consequences of those actions, but perhaps it would have deterred him from what he ended up doing to them. So, as dumb sheep being led to a slaughter, they simply obeyed Daddy's wishes and allowed themselves to be tied to the piano with the rope. I can tell you that there is absolutely no way in this world that I would have consented to that. He would have had to catch me first.

So, with one rope, he bound them to the piano, and with the other rope, he started thrashing them while repeatedly demanding a confession from who had taken his silver dollar collection. This whipping went on for what seems like a lifetime, and no one was owning up to the disappearance of that coin collection. Daddy finally realized that no one was going to confess to taking the silver dollar collection and thank God what was left of his good senses kicked in and he stopped whipping them before he seriously injured or killed them.

I could barely believe what I had just witnessed. Did he really TIE them to the piano with a rope and then beat them with another rope? Where in the world did this barbaric behavior come from? Who in the world was this man? Well, this man was my Daddy, and I still loved him. Yes, I still loved him even after seeing what he did. And then he said the strangest thing to me.

After he untied my brothers from the piano, Daddy went and sat on the steps of the front porch, and I went and sat next to him. He turned and looked at me and told me that it was going to be me the next time. I guess Daddy must have been thinking about all of the mischievous things that I had done that he allowed me to get away with and at that moment he was sending a warning to me that if I didn't get it together, I was going to feel some of his wrath too. Thankfully, that never happened.

I remember my Daddy putting his hands on me only once in my lifetime. I was having a temper tantrum one day because I couldn't get my way about something. Daddy was making a repair to the door jamb of one of the bedroom doors. Well in my fit of rage, I stomped away and slammed that same door that daddy was working on.

I had no idea that I had almost slammed Daddy's hand in the door and that infuriated him. I was in another room sulking and pouting when all of a sudden, I felt the worst stinging on one of my thighs. Daddy had quietly crept to the room that I had gone into, sneaked up on me, and with the palm of his hand, smacked the living daylights out of one of my thighs. I was startled, mad, and hurt all at the same time. That was the first and last time that I recall Daddy ever putting his hands on me. It wasn't because I didn't deserve it though. I was just a spoiled brat and often got away with my share of misdeeds.

But back to the silver dollar collection drama. Daddy eventually ended up finding his silver dollar collection. In his effort to make sure he had hidden it well to keep us prowling children from finding it, he had hidden it from himself. After accusing my brothers of being thieves and putting them through that awful whipping ordeal, he had found the silver dollars. Now you would think that he would have run to them and begged their forgiveness for first of all falsely accusing them of doing something that they clearly did not do, and secondly for the harsh punishment that he had subjected them to, but as far as I know, he never apologized to my brothers for his cruel actions.

> *"Too often, we forget that* discipline really means to teach, *not to punish. A disciple is a student, not a recipient of behavioral consequences."*
>
> (Daniel J. Siegel)

CHAPTER 6

SHE WENT OVERBOARD

Sad to say, my Daddy was not the only parent that went a little ballistic a couple of times. Mama had one or two of those moments as well. As if the things that Daddy did weren't bad enough, I had to come to grips with the fact that the one who most children look to for nurturing and protection, at times, did the exact opposite.

The more I think about it, the more I'm convinced that my parents played a role in my brothers' mental health issues. I'm positive that some of the psychological and physical pain that was inflicted on my brothers was an enormous contributing factor to the sorrowful paths of their lives.

It's not a very nice thing to say and I know that you're going to judge me for it; but I'll have to admit that while growing up as a child, I hated my Mama. I often wished that she was dead. I said to myself that if she were dead, then I wouldn't have to endure the psychological torment that she inflicted upon me on a regular basis. I don't know when it all began, but very early in life, I concluded that my Mama was not one of my favorite people, and that's probably because I felt that I was not one of her favorite people.

My Mama was a feisty one. No one ever had to guess where she was coming from because she usually told you exactly how she felt about a situation. She believed in calling things just as she saw them. Folk usually weren't too happy about this, but she didn't let that bother her. Mama was the no nonsense type, and she didn't care for a lot of foolishness. She was very opinionated, and her opinion was always right.

Even though my brothers experienced some horrifying experiences with Daddy, Mama did a lot of the disciplining in our household. For the most part, she was usually the one handing down the sentences when we disobeyed. And in my estimation, her punishment almost never fit the crime. She always went overboard when it came to discipline. She definitely ruled with an iron fist, and Mama would not ever be found guilty of "sparing the rod and spoiling the child."

Like most children, my brothers had a curfew that required them to be home at a certain hour. I would venture to say, that like most children, the curfew was sometimes violated.

But as I can recall, my brothers seemed to violate their curfew more often than not. I remember Mama locking them out of the house a few times and they had to sleep in Daddy's car. You would think that being locked out of the house and having to spend the night in the car would make them think twice about violating their curfew, but it didn't. When my brothers seemed to have become immune to being locked outside and sleeping in the car, I suppose Mama needed to come up with some other form of punishment to convince them that she was not playing games with them.

At one point, Mama began threatening to beat them with a board with nails in it if they continued to violate their curfew. Now I honestly believed, at that time, that initially she was just selling wolf tickets to try and get them to do the right thing. I didn't believe that she really had any intentions of carrying out that ridiculous threat.

But as time would tell, I realize that from the first time she uttered those words, she indeed had every intention of carrying out her threat. Come to think of it my Mama was not one for making idle threats. As I am writing this, I am saying to myself, what kind of madness could have been going on in her mind? How far down did she have to dig to produce the idea for this unorthodox method of punishment? Was she seriously thinking about beating the ones she'd carried in her womb for nine months with a board of nails? Could she have possibly thought of a more civilized way to handle their disobedience? How she managed to escape the scrutiny of the Department of Children's Service after her horrendous act, I'll never know.

My brothers couldn't seem to help themselves and continued to violate their curfew. Perhaps they really didn't believe that Mama would follow through with her threats to beat them with a board of nails, because they continued to be non-compliant. If only they'd known.

As the saying goes, "all good things must come to an end," and one night, unfortunately for my brothers, their good thing had indeed come to an end. Judgment day had finally arrived.

If they could've known what I knew about what was going to happen to them that night, they would've gone into hiding.

I couldn't believe my eyes as I watched Mama find and prepare her "punishment board." It wasn't hard for her to locate the two-by-four because our yard was filled with them. The man who owned our house was a brick mason and he often used our yard as a storage area for his surplus equipment. Mama just popped over to the place in the yard where the two-by-fours were stored and picked one for her whipping board. She painstakingly hammered nails into it so that the pointed ends protruded through to the other side. I desperately want to believe that I imagined all of this, but as God is my witness, this is the truth, the whole truth, and nothing but the truth, so help me God.

I thought it was bad enough when I was told by some of my friends that they got whippings with an extension cord, but a board with nails in it! My Mama had taken things to another level. I watched Mama's adrenaline flow as she was preparing this lethal invention of hers that she would use to punish my brothers and wished I had some way to warn my brothers to run like hell in the other direction and never come back to this house of insanity. Unfortunately, I had no way of warning them and sadly, they were just going to have to suffer some very cruel and unusual punishment for their continual disobedience. Oh, how I wished Mama would have just stuck to her old method of punishment where she would just lock them out and they would have to sleep in the car, but now that was a thing of the past. I guess you could say that Mama had had enough and was going to show my brothers who was in charge.

When my brothers finally came home, they were met by Mama brandishing a two-by-four with nails in it and regrettably, she did to them exactly what she had threatened to do. She beat them with that board! I don't remember the specifics of that drama because either I hid so I wouldn't have to witness it, or I just simply blocked it out. Perhaps this was better for me. You can only imagine what a bloody mess this ended up being. How she managed to dole out this type of punishment without them ending up in the hospital is a mystery to me to this very day.

She probably just did what I remember her doing to me once. She beat the living daylights out of me and left all kinds of whelps on me and then doctored me up so nobody would know. I remember being in such pain and needing the relief, but at the same time wishing that I had the courage to just punch her lights out while she was soothing my wounds. How dare you beat the snot out of me and then attempt to cover up the evidence! I honestly think she felt bad for what she had done, but she never uttered it from her lips.

It gets worse.

I remember coming close to losing part of one of my feet at the hands of Mama one day.

I had a habit of running away when Mama would attempt to whip me. I wasn't going down without a fight, so she always had to chase me in order to give those licks. The way our house was laid out, all of the rooms were adjoining which meant that you could enter a room through one door and exit it through a door of the room next to it and vice versa. So, basically when Mama would whip me, she would literally have to chase me in and out of all of those rooms.

Now that I think back on it, that scenario was pretty hilarious. I can picture myself running in and out of those rooms while Mama tirelessly chased after me. Of course, she always won.

One day, Mama says to me "the next time you run when I'm whipping you, I'm gonna throw that hatchet at you." Yes, you heard me right.

Well, it was sooner than later that the day came when I was up for another whipping. Although I had totally forgotten about Mama's threat to throw the hatchet at me the next time I ran while she was trying to whip me, of course, she hadn't forgotten. I know you more than likely already have a pretty good clue of how this story is going to end but let me just give you a blow-by-blow of what happened that day.

Of course, it was pretty much predictable what I would do when it was time for a whipping, so as usual I started running when Mama brought the switch out.

Mama started heading towards me and as was my custom, I bolted. This time the chase didn't last nearly as long as it usually did. I briefly weaved in and out of one or two rooms until all of a sudden, I heard a thud that stopped me dead in my tracks. I stood there frozen for just a few seconds, and when I finally turned and looked down behind me, there resting dangerously close to one of my heels was the hatchet. When I tell you that in spite of Mama's history of doing some pretty wild things, in the name of discipline, it still took me a moment to wrap my mind around the fact that this woman had actually thrown the hatchet at me! I am grateful that she aimed low because had she aimed higher, this story would have likely ended quite differently. There's a very good possibility that I could have been severely injured or even killed.

When I tell you the hatchet missed my heel by mere inches, I am not exaggerating. Had she applied just a smidgen more force when she threw that hatchet, I would have likely been missing part of a foot. I shudder to think of an artery that could have been severed and I could have bled to death. Now I don't know if she was aiming for my feet or not, but I suppose she was since the whole thing was about me running when she tried to whip me. Was my Mama really trying to take off a foot to make her point to me? All indications point to a resounding YES!

> *Discipline: to punish or penalize for the sake of enforcing obedience and perfecting moral character.*
>
> (MERRIAM-WEBSTER)

> *A large body of research shows links between corporal punishment and a wide range of negative outcomes, both immediate and long-term.*

> *Mental ill-health, including behavioral and anxiety disorders, depression, hopelessness, low self-esteem, self-harm and suicide attempts, alcohol and drug dependency, hostility, and emotional instability, which continue into adulthood.*
>
> (WORLD HEALTH ORGANIZATION)

CHAPTER 7

MAKE IT MAKE SENSE

It saddens me greatly that I'm to recalling these horrible incidents carried out by my parents. The fact of the matter is, these things happened, and I strongly believe that they greatly influenced the way my brothers and I turned out in life. I am not making excuses, just stating the facts.

Although I wish things would have turned out differently in my family, I know that everything happens for a reason. My prayer is that my story will first let others know that they are not alone, and that it will enlighten others on the subject of mental illness, especially regarding the importance of early intervention.

At one time, it was very shameful and hurtful to admit to myself how things were in my family because I suppose I was comparing my family to what I believed to be true about everyone else's family. But now I have no shame because I fully understand how what happened in my family factors into my purpose in life.

As I reflect back on growing up in the Mobley household, I can honestly say that I don't recall a lot of happy times. Mama and I didn't have a good relationship at all, and you should know by now that my

Daddy was my hero. I tried to spend every waking moment that I could with him. I even often went to work with him when I wasn't in school.

We just never were what I would consider the typical family based on how most of my friends lived, or how they appeared to live. I believed that a typical family had structure. In my mind, they shared meals, the children were responsible for chores being done according to a schedule, the parents went grocery shopping together, and there were always regular family vacations and family time. Such was not the case in my family. Everyone seemed to live in their own little world within the household.

I'm having to wrack my brain to try to remember us all being gathered around the dining room table for a meal. Mealtime in my household went something like this. Mama would cook the meal and then each one of us would take turns going in the kitchen to fix our plate and then retreat to whatever spot in the house we chose, where we would eat our meal. I suppose every now and then one or two of us would sit at the dining room table together, but never all of us at the same time. As a matter of fact, my favorite place to eat was in my bedroom sitting on my bed. And when I really think about it, that's where the siblings usually went to eat, to their bedrooms. Daddy would fuss at me about eating in my room, but I was never actually forbidden to do it.

There were times when I sat at the dining room table with Daddy, but there was not much conversation. You see I loved to read, so I would read whatever was near me as I ate. For example, I can picture that Morton salt box that was usually on the dining room table. Most of the people that I knew had a salt and pepper shaker on the table, but we literally kept the salt container on the table. I had this thing where I would read the words on the salt box as I ate. I played this game with myself where I would see how many words, I could make from the words on the salt box. For the life of me, I still don't understand why we all never sat at the table together and ate, but the fact of the matter is that we just didn't. When we were done eating, in our respective places, everyone would eventually filter into the kitchen one at a time where we would place our dish in the sink.

Since no one was assigned to wash the dishes, they may or may not have gotten washed. They could pile up for days. The fact that for many years we didn't have hot water didn't make matters easy either. You see when anyone did finally do the dishes, we would have to use one of our huge pots and heat water on the stove to make dishwater.

Maybe that explains why no one ever rushed to do the dishes. The landlord never bothered to install a hot water heater in our home. You would have thought that we were living in the stone ages. But what puzzles me is why Daddy, being the man of the house, never demanded that we have a hot water heater installed. For whatever reason, eventually the landlord decided that it was time and that's when we got a hot water heater.

I'm sure you're probably wondering what we did for bathing during the time we didn't have hot water. We did the same thing we did when we washed dishes. We would heat water on the stove and lug it from the kitchen to the bathroom and pour it in the tub. We would then run the cold water in the tub to balance out the water temperature. Nobody ever really knows what goes on behind closed doors. I can't help but think that this type of dysfunction could have very well contributed to the poor mental health of me and my siblings.

I mentioned earlier that when we were done eating, we would place our dirty dishes in the sink and sometimes they would remain there until the next day or sometimes days later. By the time someone did decide to do the dishes, the scene was not very pleasant. The sink would be filled with dirty dishes and the water that was in it would more than likely consist of some unsightly insects floating around in it.

Now I know this sounds totally disgusting, but it's the truth. Whoever decided to wash the dishes that day would just have to deal with the situation. We did what we had to do. We weren't nasty people; although

I know what I just described may cause some to question that. Our appliances always looked brand-spanking-new because Mama took extra care in making sure of that. My Mama was very clean in spite of the fact that she was a pack rat. We had a lot of stuff in our house but let me reiterate that we were not nasty people. I guess you wonder how we managed to have clean clothes since at one point we didn't have hot water. Well, this non-typical family had a remedy for that. Daddy sent his suits and work uniforms to the dry cleaners and Mama washed everything else by hand and hung them to dry on the clothesline in the backyard. Sometimes the linen got piled up and she would send that out to a laundry service. I remember that my brothers and I at times would individually take our own clothes to the coin laundry to wash, dry, and fold. Now maybe we weren't the only family living this way, but none of the homes that I visited seemed to be run like this.

Another thing was the distribution of chores. Chores? That word didn't even exist in my house. Most children were required to make their beds every day and keep their rooms tidy. This was not a requirement at my house. We hopped out of bed in the morning and left it exactly the way it was. I will have to admit that my brothers kept their rooms tidy, but my room always looked like a hurricane had swept through it. I would have those times when I just couldn't take it anymore and I would give it a thorough cleaning and organize it, which would not last a very long time. I suppose this could explain why I eventually became such a neat freak. I literally went from one end of the spectrum to the other.

Now I wish I knew the answer to why my parents didn't require more structure in our household, but this lack of discipline and structure would only work against them in the future.

I told you how my Mama had this thing about cleanliness right? Well, it was so much so that she never allowed any of us to help out in the kitchen. I remember her telling us and others, "I don't want no nasty chillen in my kitchen." You would think that since I was a girl, that she would have pulled me alongside her and taught me what most mothers teach their daughters, how to get around in the kitchen, but she didn't. When she said that she didn't want no "chillen" in her kitchen, she really meant that. She wouldn't even allow me to wash dishes. And then she wondered why the first time she told me to clean up the kitchen, I refused.

I know some of you are perplexed by the fact that I refused to do what she said, but remember, she had never really allowed me into the kitchen. Sure, I know it didn't take rocket science to wash dishes, but as a young girl, I suppose that I would have needed a little bit of guidance. I totally rebelled when she told me to wash the dishes. My thoughts were, "I haven't BEEN washing them and I'm not about to start NOW!" I just outright refused!

I don't know how it all began, but I was very rebellious and often got away with being disobedient. So that particular evening I recall her telling me to wash the dishes and when I refused, she told me that I would either wash the dishes or I would not go to bed that night. Well needless to say I accepted the challenge and refused to wash the dishes and sat up half of the night. Clearly there was some major dysfunction here where authority was concerned. With most parents, this would not have been up for discussion. In most households I would have simply done what I was instructed to do or suffered the consequences. In case you're wondering, I DID NOT wash the dishes and I went to bed.

To this day I can't explain how I was able to pull this off without getting my butt whipped. On the one hand, my parents were these militant, irrational tyrants when it came to doling out punishment; especially to my brothers, but on the other hand they were extremely passive. I guess you could say that there was no middle ground here. They were either extremely to the left or extremely to the right. For a child, this can be quite confusing.

Another consideration that I want to mention is that in my estimation what qualified us as the not so typical family was the fact that we never took family vacations, I mean never.

I know that there's no rule of thumb that says vacations are a given, but I'm just saying. I would often see our neighbors piling into their family vehicle and getting away for a few days. Never for us. The most we ever did was take a trip to Alabama or somewhere and it was usually to attend a funeral. I would hardly consider that a family vacation. Where in the world was the balance in all of this?

The only thing that I remember us doing as a family on a regular basis was going to church. I am by no means implying that there was something wrong with us going to church. All I'm saying is that too much of one thing and not enough of another can create a serious imbalance, and I would venture to say that therein lies a huge problem within our family. As far as I'm concerned, our lives were quite boring. We were expected to just digest whatever the adults were digesting, and all would be well. Well not so. That's probably the only thing my parents really made a big deal about when it came down to structure. Going to church was supposed to ward off all of the evil spirits and make us good little children. Well, if that was the case, I'd like to know how my brothers ended up the way that they did. I remember my brother Donny being the first one to start falling apart.

> *If you've grown up in a dysfunctional household, doing the work on yourself is ultimately the best place to start tackling the trauma. Sometimes finding the right counsellor takes some time. If you're looking to work on the issues brought about from dysfunctional family life, you should find a counsellor who specializes in family-focused therapy and cognitive work.*
>
> (Talkspace)

CHAPTER 8

DONNY'S DESCENT

I will never forget that frightful night when my oldest brother James stumbled inside the front door of our house with my brother Donny flung over his shoulder. Once James let Donny down to the floor, and we could see Donny's face, it was evident that Donny was totally oblivious to his surroundings. His facial expression was completely blank.

Now the average person observing this unusual behavior in an individual would probably have called 911 or immediately taken my brother to the nearest hospital, which by the way was all of five minutes away. Instead, however, Daddy says to James throw him in that back room and I'll bet he'll straighten up."

Now the "room" that Daddy was referring to, was this room that was at the very back of our house that was jam packed with practically any and every item imaginable. It was where we stored things that we didn't use. There was clothing, furniture, appliances, sporting equipment, books, bed linens, and the lists goes on and on. The room was packed from top to bottom, side to side, and from front to back. I remember trying to get in there at times (for what reason, I couldn't tell), and you would literally have to force the door open because of all of the stuff piled in there. I often said that if anyone ever broke into our home to harm us, I would take refuge in that room because they would never find me in there.

You could hide an elephant amidst all of that clutter. This was the room where James was to "throw" Donny into to cure him. And he did exactly what Daddy told him to do and literally dropped Donny in that room full of stuff. Donny stayed in that room for the rest of the night. He was out cold and clueless. By God's grace, Donny made it through the night. We later discovered that my brothers' behavior that night was because he had been under the influence of drugs. Thank God for small favors that he had not taken a huge overdose and was able to just sleep it off. I often shudder when I remember this incident thinking about how my brother could have easily severely harmed himself in that room or even died for lack of proper medical attention.

That night was probably a foretelling of the mental health slippery slope that Donny would soon begin sliding down.

Donny had been expelled from school when he was only in the eighth grade. Donny told the story, after the fact, of taking the rap for something that he didn't do which had resulted in his expulsion from school. The school he attended was hosting a basketball game one evening and it seems that after the game the kids became somewhat rowdy and in the midst of all of the chaos, a window of a school bus from the visiting team was smashed.

Donny, along with a few of his friends was accused of being the culprits and ultimately Donny was fingered as being the one who actually threw the rock that busted out the window of the bus. I can't imagine why what seemed to be a minor incident required such harsh punishment, but Donny was expelled from school for the rest of the year, and for whatever reason, the other guys were able to return to school.

The assistant principal of that school, who was a good friend to Daddy, stopped by the house one evening shortly after this happened to discuss Donny's expulsion with my parents. He believed that for Donny to be expelled was drastic and unfair. He had come to encourage Daddy to visit the school to appeal that decision. Daddy's friend advised him if he would come to the school and fight the decision that chances were that Donny's sentence could possibly be reduced from expulsion to suspension.

Now I know you probably wonder how I can remember some of the details that I share with you in this book, but trust me, I have a good memory and seemed to always be lurking when there was interesting adult conversation taking place, especially if it involved Daddy.

Sadly, Daddy did not take his friend's advice to go to the school and fight for Donny, and unfortunately Donny was out of school for the remainder of the year, and ultimately forever. He was an official, dropout. At some point Donny decided to enroll in the Job Corps and left our hometown of Panama City for a while. While in the Job Corps Donny became certified as a chef and upon completion of his time in the Job Corps returned home. I remember all of the great tasting dishes that he would prepare for our family.

It appeared that things had taken a good turn for Donny, and he was on the right path. He was dating a very attractive girl who he was head-over-heels in love with, and his affection was reciprocated by her. She drove a green Chevy Malibu; she drove like a bat out of hell. She would often come by our house to pick me up and take me for rides. Mama would often warn me to stay out of the car with her because Mama thought she drove too fast, but I just loved being around her and I wouldn't stay out of the car with her. Even though her driving raised the hair on my body, and I was as scared as all get-out when I rode with her, it didn't stop me from hanging out with her. There was a period of time that she didn't have brakes and would slam on her emergency brake to stop the car.

Thankfully, I lived through riding in the car with my brother's reckless girlfriend. There's an old saying that "God looks out for babies and fools." I certainly wasn't a baby, so I guess I must've been a fool.

Donny eventually decided to take the relationship to the next level and one Christmas he proposed to his girlfriend and gave her an engagement ring. The ring was too big and needed to be sized, but she wore it anyway. One day Donny asked for the ring to take it to have it sized. A long period of time passed, and he never returned the ring to her. In the meantime, Donny decided to take a trip to Miami to visit our aunt and was there for a short period. He was in constant communication with his fiancé at first and then suddenly, the phone calls became far and few between. It seems as though the distance was making the heart grow yonder and not fonder on Donny's part. He eventually stopped accepting her phone calls. I know this because she told me.

After a period of time, he finally accepted a phone call from her, and during that call, he dealt her a devastating blow. He said he no longer wanted to marry her. My aunt called Mama and told her that she needed to send Donny money for a bus ticket to come home because he was no longer welcome in Miami. It seems that he was exemplifying some strange behavior. Mama sent Donny money for a bus ticket to come back home but he didn't come back right away as expected. Mama called her sister to find out what was going on and was told that Donny must have never purchased the bus ticket to return home and may have used the money for something else.

We never discovered what the something else was. My aunt asked Mama to send money again for a bus ticket but told Mama to send the money to her this time instead of Donny. Mama sent more money for a bus ticket and the story goes that my aunt had to go and purchase the bus ticket and literally go with Donny to the bus station to make sure that he boarded the bus. Now no one really knew what was going on except that Donny was displaying some extremely bizarre behavior.

Thank God that whatever was going on with Donny didn't prevent him from making it back home that time. As strangely as he was behaving, he somehow knew to not to get off the bus until he reached home. Donny finally made it back home, and we were not prepared for what we saw.

He literally looked like he'd been sleeping on the streets. He was very unkempt, and something was definitely not right. Donny was known for being one of the most well-dressed among his peers. He always looked like he had just stepped out of GQ Magazine and had a swagger about himself that put him a cut above the rest. Everything he wore had to be ironed with all of the creases in the right places. His clothes were always perfectly matched. Let's just say that he was always impeccably dressed.

But the moment Donny showed up at the front door of our house from his trip to Miami, everyone could immediately see that something was terribly wrong. The person I just described as always being impeccably dressed was looking like a complete stranger. His facial expressions were just blank. There was no life in his countenance. As he walked past us, we could see that the back stitching of his pants was ripped wide open. Although he left home with a suitcase full of clothes, he had only a few items in his luggage.

It wasn't just these external signs that indicated that there was something terribly wrong with my brother, it was the look in his eyes that let us know that the Donny that left for Miami a few weeks ago was not the same Donny that returned home. Looking into his eyes was like looking into empty holes. There was nothing there. He just had this glazed-over look. We saw a body that was moving about, but the once vibrant person that we had known was clearly gone. He was never much of a talker and now he was talking even less.

When his fiancé heard that Donny had made it back to town she hurried to our house because she was extremely excited that he had returned home. There was nothing that could have prepared her for the huge surprise that she received.

Her excitement was very short-lived when she realized that her welcome home to Donny was met with little to no reaction. You would have thought she was a complete stranger because that's exactly how Donny treated her. He showed very little emotion and had we not known any better, we would have thought he had no idea who she was. It was very tough for us to watch her as she attempted to relate to Donny as she had done before he left for Miami.

That blank look in his eyes that did not remotely reflect that he had ever had any attachment to her. As hard as she tried to make things right, her efforts failed. It didn't take her long to realize that this was not the same man who had been gone for just a short while. No one suspected that tragically Donny would never be the same again.

The question then became, what in the world happened to Donny while he was in Miami? We never found out for sure what happened but could only speculate. My aunt told us that while he was visiting Miami he had been doing fine until one night he went out but returned home acting very strange. Her guess was that he had perhaps left a drink unattended only to have someone slip some type of drug into his drink when he wasn't looking and that's what could have started this whole mess.

This explanation was not very far-fetched because this type of activity was very common during that time. Whatever the case was, all we know is that Donny left Panama City one way and returned a totally different person.

I remember in the weeks following his return home, Donny would sit glued to one spot, chain smoking cigarettes and talking to himself most of the day. Now you would have thought that my parents would have tried to get some type of help for him, but they didn't, and things just ended up going from bad to worse. Did they really think that this was just going to go away? I suppose him displaying this abnormal behavior inside the house was one thing, but after a while, he decided to take it outside.

Donny decided one day that he would start walking with me to school. Mind you, at this point in time, I am in high school, and the school was approximately a one and a half mile walk from our home. Now the fact that Donny wanted to walk with me to school was not the issue. The problem came with what he chose to wear when he would walk me to school. During that time, if someone asked for the definition of mortified, certainly a picture of me would have provided the perfect example. To this day, I still wonder what I did to deserve that humiliation. Remember, Donny had returned from Miami with virtually no clothes.

The white folks that Mama worked for would often give her either brand new or gently worn clothing. So almost every day that she came home from work, she would have either one or several bags of clothing that they'd given her. The clothes were always nice, but occasionally we would find some outdated pieces. These clothes would be in mint condition. Not only that, but the clothing items were almost always unmistakably for women.

The day that Donny decided to start walking with me to school, lo-and-behold if he didn't step out of his room with a woman's pants suit on. What in the world was going on here? One might think that it would have been easy for me to decline his offer to walk with me to school that day, but I have a feeling this would have been much easier said than done. He was going to walk me to school, end of story.

I marvel at myself when I think of how amazing it is that almost fifty years later, I can perfectly describe the outfit that he wore that day. The pants suit was made of double-knit fabric with faint squares in the fabric and was of mixed rust colors with a solid rust trim. The jacket was cardigan style that was sleeveless and since he was short in stature, the bottom of the jacket probably hit Donny somewhere around the knees. I can't remember what type of shirt he wore underneath…probably a woman's blouse, or what type of shoes he wore, but it was quite obvious that this man was wearing a woman's pantsuit.

Nowadays that may not seem very strange, but back then, it was very strange. I was shocked to see him wearing this outfit, and even though I was clearly embarrassed that he would be wearing this ridiculous outfit while walking me to school, there was nothing I could do about it. Due to his mental state, it would have been absolutely pointless for me to say anything. He repeated this for several days, and I endured the humiliation. And then one day as abruptly as it began, it stopped. All I could say was thank you Jesus. For some reason I can't recall my friends' reaction when they saw this (maybe I purposely blocked this out), but I'm sure I must have been the laughingstock of the school. My brother was never "right" again, and I guess you could say that he was certifiably crazy.

What are the causes of mental illness? Although the exact cause of most mental illnesses is not known, it is becoming clear through research that many of these conditions are caused by a combination of biological, psychological, and environmental factors.

(WebMD)

CHAPTER 9

THE DESCENT OF BROTHER #2

Meanwhile, there were still my other two brothers, James, and Dwight, who both were starting to show signs of having mental health issues. It looks like this mental health thing was starting to pick my brothers off one at a time. At first, things seemed to be rolling along just fine for James. He had graduated from high school and had continued working at Rogers Chrysler Plymouth as a mechanic's apprentice. He had worked for them after school while he was still a student. Managing to save up enough money to buy himself a car, he purchased a navy-blue Volkswagen with gangsta-white-wall tires, and a sunroof top, and things were seemingly going well for him.

James had a girlfriend whose name coincidently was the same as my brother Donny. She was a cutie, and she just adored James. I remember her being very petite. I chuckle when I recall the times that she and James would talk on the telephone for hours and sometimes I would walk past his room to see the phone dangling from his ear, and he would be snoring like a bear. Sometimes I could overhear her calling out to him, or she would have hung up the phone and all that could be heard was a dial tone.

Back in those days my brother decided to shave his head bald, having been inspired by that great singer, actor, songwriter, and composer Isaac Hayes. Amazingly, James bore a very striking resemblance to Isaac Hayes. So much so that shortly after shaving his head, he was hanging out at Panama City Beach one day and word began spreading throughout town like wildfire that Isaac Hayes was on the beach. You can imagine what an uproar that caused? Of course, my brother got a big kick out of having his few hours of instant fame.

Life was moving along pretty normal for James until one day his past sins, if you will, began catching up to him. Not only that, but I was later told by an older cousin that James suffered from stomach issues as a young child. So, while still in high school and after graduating, he and his boys would spend time hanging out by the corner store drinking booze. They weren't bothering anyone. This was their pastime and they enjoyed it. Who could imagine what this would eventually lead to for my brother James? We all know that alcohol is bad for you when you're abusing it, but until then, I had never thought of him as someone abusing alcohol. I just saw it as some guys hanging on the corner enjoying each other's company.

The first sign that there was something going on with James was when Mama found him passed out in the back room one evening. No, he hadn't passed out from drinking. At that time, we didn't know why he had passed out. There would be several more of these episodes before it dawned on Mama that there was a problem. He saw a doctor, and it was determined that James was suffering from a bleeding ulcer. He had been losing a lot of blood, so it made sense that he had been passing out. He was losing a lot of blood on a regular basis which caused his blood count to become critically low and subsequently he would pass out. This had gone on for quite some time before medical attention was sought, and by the time he saw a doctor, his condition had worsened to the point of needing a surgical procedure pretty quickly. Although James was in severe constant pain every day, the idea of having surgery did not set too well with him. It took quite a bit of convincing to get him to consent to having the surgery before he finally agreed to it. Everyone breathed a sigh of relief because it was a very good chance that the surgery would give him back some quality of life, which had diminished considerably because of his illness.

On the day that James was scheduled to have surgery, he changed his mind. Right before the anesthesia was to be administered, James abruptly changed his mind and refused to go through with the operation. My brother literally walked away from the hospital without having the surgery.

That was probably one of the worst decisions that he could have ever made. After that, not only would his physical health take a turn for the worse, but eventually his mental health would suffer as well. We knew that James was in critical need of that surgery for the bleeding ulcer, but there was nothing that anyone could do to convince him to have the surgery. He made his decision. No one was really aware of how this bleeding ulcer was taking a toll on James' mental health because he managed to keep some parts of his suffering under the radar.

One symptom that was prominent as a result of the bleeding ulcer was frequent vomiting. By and by, it was discovered that James had been sneaking outside of the house to vomit in order to keep us from knowing. Once we found out, he stopped going outside to vomit and just started going inside. He would use a mop bucket to vomit in, and the amount that would be released was unthinkable.

There was not much that anybody could do. We just had to stand helplessly by and watch my brother suffer. As badly as James was suffering, he continued to refuse to have the surgery. One of my most vivid recollections of seeing how badly my brother was suffering was watching him crawl on his knees, clutching his mid-section as he cried like a baby because he was in so much pain. That image will be forever etched in my mind.

With this type of illness, James was missing a lot of work and although he was a star player on the team at Rogers Chrysler-Plymouth, at some point, they had no choice but to terminate his employment. I remember James being devastated by his termination because now he had no income and one thing led to another. He had taken pride in being able to be independent and self-sufficient. He had moved away from home at some point, but when his health continued failing and he lost his income, he was forced to move back home. He would have his good days and bad days, but it got to the point where I would say that ninety-five percent of his days were bad.

As his physical health steadily declined, his mental health began steadily declining as well. He was eventually diagnosed with what was known at that time as manic depression. Manic depression is a disorder associated with episodes of mood swings ranging from depressive lows to manic highs. It seems that in James' case, his mood was usually that of depressive lows. He would sit around all day long just holding his stomach with his head bowed. He would only move from his spot on the sofa when it was absolutely necessary.

At that point, we had two mentally ill siblings under the same roof. The problem wasn't that they had mental health issues, but the problem was, they weren't being treated. There was a storm brewing, and we weren't prepared for it.

One day a fight broke out between James and Donny. I don't know what sparked it, but it ended up being very intense. They were rumbling so badly that one or two of the legs of Mama's practically brand-new dining room table were broken when one of my brothers threw the other against the table. It seemed like this fight would never end. If Daddy had been at home when it started, I doubt the fight would have gone on quite as long.

At some point Daddy came home and they were still fighting, and he had to intervene to stop them from fighting. Sadly, in the heat of the moment and in the midst of this melee, Daddy somehow ended up getting punched in the stomach by James.

Finally, the fight ended but not before there had been damage done to property as well as to people. The dining room table was eventually repaired, but the psychological damage that James suffered as a result of punching Daddy in the stomach was something that James would never get over. I'm not sure how long after this incident occurred that Daddy passed away, but after his passing James confessed that he had never apologized to Daddy for punching him in the stomach during his and Donny's fight. James was very remorseful about this, but because Daddy died without James ever apologizing to him, he suffered a huge emotional toll. It got so bad that James ended up sinking into a mental abyss from which he would never recover.

Regrettably, the rest of his life would be spent in and out of the local mental health unit and the state hospital. James' mood was usually pretty low, and he would occasionally erupt into explosive behavior which could be very scary. Sadly, there were a couple of times that James' outbursts were provoked. I can only imagine the mental torment my brother must have been experiencing on a regular basis. To have this torment coupled with, at times, agitation and instigation was only a recipe for disaster.

Sadly, our Mama was often responsible for the agitation and the instigation. Why she was unable to see how her ill-judged behavior would adversely affect my brother, I will never know. To this day I still remain completely baffled by her insistence upon pressing the issues that would obviously cause James to snap, but somehow, she was unable to restrain herself from being a troublemaker.

I wish she were here right now. She would never admit that she was at fault for some of James' outbursts, but I sure would still like to ask what had been the source of and method to her madness.

> *There's a strong relationship between physical and mental health conditions. People with chronic physical illnesses are twice as likely to suffer from anxiety or depression as their physically healthy counterparts—and for specific health conditions, the rate is even higher.*
>
> (BLACK BEAR LODGE)

CHAPTER 10

SHE WOULDN'T STOP

I am thinking of one incident that Mama provoked that ended up creating a major ruckus one evening and miraculously no one was seriously injured.

On this particular evening, dusk had settled in, when the drama began. Everything was quiet on the set when suddenly Mama went to the front door and stood there for a few moments peering out into the darkness and then started repeatedly saying that someone was watching our house. What I know now that I didn't know then is that Mama too had some mental health issues.

She continually repeated that someone was watching our house and one of the few peaceful evenings that we were managing to enjoy was slowing turning into something that none of us had foreseen. Now mind you, across the street from our house in an otherwise empty field stood a huge oak tree and under that tree our next-door neighbor had placed an old wooden bench for sitting. You would quite often find him just sitting on the old wooden bench relaxing and puffing on his pipe.

I knew that it was our neighbor out there sitting on the bench since I was standing at our screen door watching him as he left his house, which was next door to ours, and walk across the street to sit on the bench.

For some odd reason, Mama kept insisting that the person sitting on the bench was some stranger and for reasons unknown to her or anyone else, this stranger had made it their business to watch our house. Now first of all, my question was why would some stranger be across the street watching our house and second of all, why wouldn't Mama believe me when I insisted that it was our neighbor out there? After this exchange went on for a few minutes, I started noticing that the more Mama insisted that some stranger was out there watching our house, the more agitated James became.

I did my best to convince her who it was over there, but she just refused to believe me. And then it happened! All of a sudden James yelled these accusatory words at me, "You know who it is, you know who it is. It's one of yo niggas!!!" I was sitting on the sofa cradling my son in my arms who was probably less than a year old at the time.

You see, after graduating from high school, I discovered I was pregnant. By the time I realized I was pregnant, I was nearing the end of my first trimester. I know you must be wondering why I didn't know before then that I was pregnant. Even though I was doing what it took to get pregnant, it never occurred to me that I was. I remember all of a sudden feeling nauseated quite often and missing my period, but DUH, it didn't hit me until one day while I was reading one of those True Confession books that the light came on.

To this day, I can remember the exact words that I read, and I quote; "When I couldn't keep anything down, I KNEW I was pregnant." My mouth immediately flew open, and I jumped up from where I was sitting. I called my best friend at the time and told her that I thought I might be pregnant. The first thing she said was, "you'd better get to the doctor!" Long story short, I did go to the doctor, and I was pregnant, and at the age of eighteen, my son was born.

When James yelled those words out to me, I angrily responded to him. I'm not sure what I said, but I probably should've used my better judgment and just kept my mouth shut. Whatever my response was to him just ticked him off and before I could blink, he leaped on me and began wildly punching me.

Since I was holding my son, he was not only punching me, but he was punching my son too. In a split-second things began spiraling out of control. I was trying to fight James off to keep him from harming me and my child and instinctively, to prevent James from harming me and my son, my brother Donny came to our rescue.

Donny grabbed the metal hose from the vacuum cleaner and started hitting James to get him off of me. I vaguely remember the sequence of events that followed, but what I do remember clearly; is that we didn't seem to be getting the best of James, so Donny and I, while holding tightly onto my child decided that it was time to get out of the house. We managed to escape James' clutches and get out of the house.

We started running away from the house. James was not going to be outdone and was determined to take out his anger on somebody. He turned his attention away from me and Donny and focused on the one who was within his reach. That person happened to be my brother Dwight who was in the bathroom shaving and was either totally oblivious to what was happening in the living room, or he somehow didn't think that he would be affected. Well, he indeed was affected because in James' rage, he stormed into the bathroom and lashed out at Dwight who had nothing to do with what was going on. They got into a scuffle and since Dwight still had the razor in his hand, he ended up getting cut with that razor. Dwight decided he'd better get out of there and managed to get past James and out of the house.

At that point, all of us had managed to get out of the house, leaving James inside. Even Mama, the instigator, had to leave because at this point, none of us, not even Mama was safe. The neighbors must have caught wind that there was a disturbance at our house, and someone called the police who showed up at the scene. This was not their first time having to come to our house and they were familiar with James and knew he had mental health issues.

By the time the police arrived, James, had barricaded himself in the house and the police began trying to coax him out. Try as they could to get him out peacefully, it was just not working. The police stood outside for what seemed like an eternity, trying to persuade James to come out, but he refused. Eventually, they had no choice but to forcefully enter the home, and so they did.

As our family, along with some of the neighbors tensely watched from the street in front of our house to see what would happen, we started hearing a loud rumbling noise coming from inside the house. The police bum-rushed the house and attempted to apprehend James. Based on the volume of the sounds coming from inside the house, everyone could tell that James was not coming out of the house without a struggle. After a brief scuffle, the policed finally subdued James, brought him out, and placed him in a police cruiser to transport him to the emergency room. Everyone breathed a sigh of relief that James had been taken from the house unharmed.

We were also relieved that everyone else was out of harm's way. Unfortunately for me, however, although James was no longer a threat to me, I would very soon realize that I had other things to be concerned about. Now what happened next totally took me by surprise.

Before the cops could drive away, Mama approached them and said to them as she nodded in my direction, "I don't want her back in my house because she started all of this."

My mouth flew open in total disbelief. Was I hearing her correctly? Did she just say that I had been the one responsible for James flipping out? You could have bought me for a penny! As hard as I tried, I was not able to convince the police that I was in no way at fault for the disturbance that had occurred earlier. My attempts to persuade them were pointless and just went in one ear and out the other. The police just blew me off because they believed what Mama said.

One officer politely said to me, "Mam, I'm sorry but you're going to have to find somewhere to go, your mother says that she doesn't want you back in her house."

Well with the cops backing Mama, it was apparent that I had no choice but to try and find some place for me and my son to lay our heads that night. By that time, it was around nine or ten o'clock at night and for the first time in my life or maybe the second, I was being put out of my Mama's house. But not just me. Remember I had a baby boy who was going right along with me.

I was simply dumbfounded, but more importantly, I was truly scared. As I stood there still in absolute disbelief, one of the neighbors came over to me and said "baby, you can come to my house." Now mind you, this wasn't one of our long-time neighbors who I had grown up with this was a family who had just recently moved into the neighborhood who I knew absolutely nothing about. What was I to do? Either I could go with the unknown or make my bed outside for the night. I went to my neighbor's house and let me just say that the experience proved to be one of the most unpleasant that I can recall. I'm almost tempted to say that I would have rather slept outside. Call me ungrateful if you will, but I'm just telling the truth. Now we were just as poor as the next family in my neighborhood, but there were certain standards that we maintained when it came down to cleanliness. My Mama may have been a hoarder, but she believed in cleanliness. Our house wasn't spotless, but it was clean. All I can say is that I have never been exposed to sleeping in a bed reeking with the smell of pee. I guess it beats what my alternative would have been. My neighbor was the sweetest person you could have ever met. She was a single mama with a house full of children and they were one happy bunch. But the way they were living was not what I was used to. Funny that our house was halfway decent to look at on the inside but was filled with a bunch of basket cases.

On the other hand, this family's house was not in the best condition, but the love and respect that they showed toward one another was second to none. To this day, I remain very grateful to our neighbor for preventing me and my baby from sleeping outside that night. I eventually fell asleep and couldn't have been happier when morning came.

I got up promptly the next morning and thanked this kind lady for her generosity in sharing her home with me the night before. Now I was on a mission. My mission was to return home that day and to not have to spend another night away from my insane but familiar surroundings. I figured that without the guys in blue at Mama's disposal, I would have a very good chance of convincing her to let me come back home. Besides, I was hoping that she had softened a bit overnight. I also thought of something else which gave me the courage that I needed to return home.

I had a memory of an incident that happened with my brother Donny back in the day before his illness. I don't recall all of the details of the incident, but I do remember the bottom line. I guess Florence Mobley was notorious for throwing you out of her house and on that occasion, it was Donny who had been thrown out. The part that stuck with me was that after being gone for a day or two, Donny showed back up on our doorstep and boldly announced that he was coming back home and was not going anywhere.

I guess Mama had softened by that time because she didn't resist and let him come back home. Well, I thought to myself, if Donny could get away with it, then it was worth a try for me. After all, what did I have to lose? Besides that, I was quite sure that if Mama refused to let me back in, I was fairly confident that the nice neighbor would let me stay at her house again. Like Donny, I showed up at the doorstep (after Mama had left for work), and when she returned home, there I was. I didn't have the guts to tell her that I wasn't going anywhere, but I just let the fact that I had returned speak for itself. I was very humble and as quiet as a church mouse. I made it my business to remain on my best behavior because I was determined to stay at home.

I guess Mama sensed that I was trying really hard to get back into her good graces and she didn't say a word one way or the other about me being back at home. As the saying goes, silence gives consent, and I took that for what it was worth. Things were still somewhat tense for a few hours, but eventually I realized that spending the night in my own bed was not going to be an issue. All was well. But not really. I was back at home, and there was still the craziness to contend with.

Agitation is a common and difficult problem in psychiatric patients; patients with bipolar disorder constitute a substantial proportion of the agitated psychiatric population. Agitation is often seen in bipolar patients during acute manic states, when increased energy levels and reduced need for sleep lead patients to collide with the limits of others. Agitation also occurs during mixed and depressive states, which are characterized by fluctuating energy levels and periods of irritability.

(National Library of Medicine)

CHAPTER 11

LIGHTNING STRIKES AGAIN

Rambunctious and extroverted are the two words that come to mind when I think of my youngest brother Dwight. Of the four siblings, I would have to say that he probably presented the most challenges to my parents. Although Dwight was very well liked by most people, his temperament was such that if you happened to end up on his wrong side, you could easily and quickly stop liking him. He rarely provoked a confrontation, but if anyone ever decided to provoke him, he was quick to defend himself.

His appearance was quite deceiving. He was average height and had a very slender build, and he was as cute as any girl I knew. He was often referred to as a "sissy." However, unfortunately for some, they had to find out the hard way that Dwight was not anybody's sissy. I can't ever remember him being in a fight where he did not come out on top. I'll have to admit that he didn't always fight fair, and let's just say that he did whatever it took to win.

Dwight was the type who was always true to himself and never pulled punches with folk. What you saw was what you got. Because of his feisty personality, it was not easily recognizable when Dwight began showing signs of mental illness. We just thought he was being who he was. Little did we know, mental illness was, lightning striking for the third time in our family.

Of all the siblings, where music was concerned, Dwight was the one that really took his music seriously.

He loved playing the piano and to help him perfect his skills Mama made him take piano lessons. Like most youngsters, I'm sure he would have rather been outside playing on those afternoons that he had piano lessons, rather than being cooped up in some house banging on a piano with some old eccentric piano instructor. Clearly, he wasn't too happy about those lessons and eventually convinced Mama to release him from that confinement.

Although he stopped taking piano lessons, Dwight didn't stop playing the piano. He was a natural. When he played piano for the choir at church, everyone enjoyed him not only because he was a gifted musician, but because of the high energy he brought to each rehearsal and church service. While in high school, Dwight got a job. With some of his earnings, he decided to invest in some musical instruments. He bought a keyboard and a guitar and spent hours on end polishing his musical talents.

He not only played instruments but was also an avid listener of music and he loved singing. Dwight owned a hefty record collection and took great pride in it. He rarely let anyone get too close to his records.

His bedroom was in the back of the house and somewhat isolated which made it possible for him to practice his music without disturbing the rest of the household. His bedroom was also the largest bedroom in the house, so he was able to turn part of it into a music studio of sorts. He would spend hours on end listening to music, writing music, and practicing singing. He invested in a tape recorder and started recording his music. After a while, all of Dwight's hard work and dedication to his music led him to dreams of someday becoming famous. He had it all figured out. He was going to eventually make it big in the music industry and his fame would spread abroad. It was just a matter of time before he would graduate from high school... Once he graduated, he would be free to pursue his dream of producing the next hit record.

Shortly after graduating from high school, and completely against Mama's wishes, Dwight packed a few of his belongings and headed downtown for the Greyhound Bus Station. He promptly set out for the big city of New York with music in tow to stake his claim to fame. I suppose next to no plan is a poorly thought-out plan. Unfortunately for Dwight, he would much sooner than later, experience the effects of the latter.

He reached the big city only to find his big dreams not remotely as he had expected. He had not done his homework and did not understand how things operated within the music industry. He was particularly naïve about how stiff the competition could be.

To his surprise, he didn't even make it to square one. The other piece that he failed to address in his preparation for stardom was plan B. He had only purchased a one-way bus ticket and didn't have much extra money. When things didn't pan out as expected, he was left stranded in the big city with no money to purchase a bus ticket to get back home.

Most likely a simple telephone call to Mama would have easily solved Dwight's money problems. He must not have been thinking straight, as he decided to hitchhike from New York City back to Florida. This would prove to be one of the worst decisions he could have ever made in life. This decision would forever change the trajectory of his life.

Dwight never personally shared with me what happened during his journey back to Florida, so this account of his experience actually came from Mama. Mama told me that as Dwight was hitchhiking back to Florida that at some point he encountered several white men in a pickup truck, and they offered him a ride.

She told the story of Dwight hopping onto the bed of the truck and falling asleep during the ride. What happened next sounds like something straight out of a thriller movie. As Mama told it to me, Dwight awakened and found himself surrounded by the men who had picked him up. They all were holding double barreled shotguns and Dwight found himself staring directly down the barrels of those shotguns. I don't know if it was instinct or if he was told to do so by the men, but according to Mama, Dwight jumped off the bed of the truck and started running away from them as fast as he could. Now this had to be about torture because it is obvious that if they had wanted to harm him at that moment either or all of them could have very easily pulled a trigger and that would have been the end of Dwight.

Such was not the case so it seems they wanted to see him sweat. I was told that they had stopped near a very heavily wooded area and Dwight was chased down into the woods by the men. We will never know if either the men lost sight of Dwight in the woods or if they just decided to let him go.

At any rate, he ended up escaping them because thank God, he lived to tell the story. He arrived safely back home, but regrettably, just like my brother Donny who was never the same again after his return home from Miami, Dwight was never the same again after returning back home from New York City.

You would think that my parents would have learned some lessons by this time. At that point, my family was three deep into this whole mental health problem.

The thing that bothers me the most right now is the fact that my brothers were in dire need of medical attention and for whatever reason or reasons, they did not get it when needed.

I recall hearing Mama saying things like, "They need to pray," "They need the Lawd," and "They need to go to church." Well, yes, I'm a firm believer in prayer, the Lord, and attending church; however, these practices of allowing them to stand alone, clearly were not the answer to my brothers' needs. My brothers needed prayer, the Lord, and the church coupled with professional treatment.

I'm inclined to believe that the reason my parents did not seek the professional help my brothers so desperately needed was because of the stigma attached to mental health disorders. No one was willing to talk outside of the family about what was going on. The embarrassment and shame trumped the stark reality that my brothers were experiencing serious mental health issues. The lack of early intervention ensured their stories would not have a happy ending.

At some point, two of my brothers, James, and Dwight, would end up receiving professional help, but not because of the prompting of my parents and not before their illness had wreaked awful havoc on our family. The truth of the matter is that, at times, their volatile behavior had called for intervention from law enforcement. As a result of law enforcement witnessing their unusual behavior, at last, my brothers received the help that they so desperately needed, but regrettably, it was too little too late. The result of these mental health issues existing untreated for so long; they were too far gone. At this stage, my brothers would most likely live out their remaining years plagued by mental health challenges. It didn't have to be this way.

James faded into the background and only occasionally had outbursts. Donny became the transient of the family. He would be here today and gone tomorrow. We never knew when he would disappear, and we never knew when he would reappear.

Dwight ended up becoming the main focus because he frequently caused disruptions. Whether it was inside of our home or within the community, he somehow managed to be the key player in some sort of ruckus regularly. You could say that inside the home he was considered the problem child and outside of the home, he could be considered a menace to society. It seemed that Dwight could not go anyplace without creating some type of commotion.

One such incident occurred on a day when he went to the Food Stamp Office to apply for assistance and was told that he was ineligible to receive food stamps. This denial apparently triggered a negative reaction in Dwight, and he just outright lost it. I was told by a friend who happened to be employed at the Food Stamp Office that Dwight turned that Food Stamp Office out after being denied assistance. She said that he became so enraged that he began picking up chairs and throwing them. Thank goodness no one was injured and Dwight somehow managed to walk away without being subdued by the authorities. That was one of the numerous times that he would be responsible for creating a public disturbance and it was all because he was suffering from a mental disorder.

Another incident that happened was when Dwight walked into a convenience store and took several food items from the shelves that he consumed on the spot and then he attempted to bypass the cashier. Of course, he was confronted by the cashier and at that point, he became extremely belligerent and began threatening to kill the cashier and her family members.

The police were called, and Dwight was taken to the local hospital's mental health unit.

That was just one of countless events that occurred where Dwight would create a disturbance, the police would be called, and he would subsequently end up in the mental health unit at the local hospital. The mental health unit for Dwight had become a revolving door.

Typically, he would create a boisterous disturbance in public, the police would be called, he would be taken to the mental health unit and admitted, remain there for 72 hours, and get released. Upon his release, he would always receive instructions to follow up with the Guidance Clinic for the continued monitoring of his medication, but he almost never complied. I'm confident he was in and out of that mental health unit several times a month.

His condition eventually worsened to the point that a stay in the local mental health unit became ineffective. He had grown accustomed to the protocol and decided that he would not comply with the regimen that was required during his 72- hour admission. This non-compliant behavior left the staff with no other choice other than the next step which required being transferred to the state hospital.

Everyone really believed that a visit to the state hospital would be just the thing to bring some order back into Dwight's life. After spending a few weeks at the state hospital, Dwight was released to come home. He showed signs of improvement and we felt very good about that. He even made sure to keep his appointments at the guidance clinic. I will never forget his case worker at the clinic. She soon became very fond of Dwight, and he was mutually fond of her. The outlook for Dwight was looking great; it appeared that he would finally be okay. He even became gainfully employed, a clear indication that he really was going to be okay.

We were sorely disappointed and very apprehensive when we noticed that a pattern began with Dwight missing his appointments at the guidance clinic. Knowing where this was leading, we strapped on our seat belts and braced ourselves for the worse. Things didn't take a turn for the worse right away and that was because his case worker took it upon herself to seek Dwight out by conducting home visits. That gesture from her was very instrumental in Dwight maintaining his stability. Over a period of time, however, Dwight became very defiant with the case worker. He began to refuse to see her at all and totally disregarded her attempts to have him follow his treatment plan.

He eventually crashed and burned and the vicious cycle of admissions to the mental health unit and the state hospital began all over again.

I thought the more intense nature of treatment inside of the state hospital would have yielded more positive results, but it finally dawned on us that no amount of treatment could help an individual without their cooperation. Such was the case with Dwight. He was just a very non-compliant type of guy which made most attempts at stabilizing his condition futile. So, the state hospital ended up becoming a revolving door for Dwight again.

Eventually, the Mobley household had gone into full-blown craziness! I can boldly say that now, but back then you had to whisper it when you said the "c" word. It had gotten so bad that what was being said about my family was, "They are all crazy." It was quite offensive to me at the time to have been labeled part of the house of the crazies, but for real for real, it was the stone-cold truth.

We would seemingly get one of the brothers under control and then another one would flip out. They took turns, there was always intense drama at 1002 East 9th Court.

Early intervention refers to recognizing the warning signs of a mental health or substance use challenge and acting before it gets worse. When you realize the signs and symptoms of a mental health challenge early, it may be easier to get appropriate help from a counselor or medical professional before it becomes worse.

Studies have shown that proper care and treatment make complete recovery from a mental health or substance use challenge attainable.

Early intervention can also save a person and their loved ones from stress, prevent more serious symptoms from developing, and reduce the likelihood of problems with work, family, school, and substance use. Plus, it could help reduce medical costs and the overall burden on friends and family members.

(MENTAL HEALTH FIRST AID USA)

CHAPTER 12

I WAS RESCUED

It looked like madness had come to my home to stay, and I really didn't want to live there anymore.

I had become a young adult and could very well have made the decision to move away. I decided not to move away because I had no financial obligations while living at home. I was receiving free room and board, so why would I move? Had it not been for the continuous drama with my brothers, I could have been living on easy street.

I finally decided that free room and board was not worth the frequent drama that I was dealing with at home, so I moved away. Free at last, or so I thought. The problem is, I ended up back at home after only being gone a short while. I made several attempts to live on my own, but my moves were always very short-lived because, honestly, I was young and extremely irresponsible during that time. I always ended up right back at home and had to deal with the madness. You would think that just the mere thought of having to live in that type of environment would cause me to get my act together and find myself a permanent residence away from there, but not so. So, once again I was back at home, and it wasn't long before *all hell broke loose.*

It was one of the last incidents that I can recall, this time it earned Dwight a pretty lengthy stay in the state hospital.

I let someone convince me to learn to roller skate at the age of twenty-two. We started going to the roller rink and it was not long before I got the hang of roller skating. Things were moving along just fine until one evening at the rink someone pulled a stupid stunt on me. I don't know what possessed this girl to do what she did, but her actions that evening created more problems for me than I had bargained for.

I was rolling along just fine, no pun intended, when she skated up behind me and gently kicked one of my feet. I lost my balance and hit the floor. It did not take very long to realize that as a result of this girl's stupid, mischievous actions; I had incurred a serious injury to my right ankle.

Within a matter of seconds, my ankle had swollen so severely that when those coming to my rescue attempted to remove the skate from my foot, it would barely budge. With a lot of manipulation and me having to endure some incredible pain, we were finally able to get the skate off my foot. When I tried to stand up, I immediately realized that I was unable to put any pressure on my right foot. I was forced to hobble off the roller rink floor with the aid of a person on either side of me because I literally was unable to walk unassisted.

Although I was in excruciating pain and couldn't put any pressure on my foot, I didn't immediately go to the hospital. Before going home, the person who had convinced me to take up roller skating took me to her house and gave me a pair of crutches that she had on hand from a recent surgery. With the aid of the crutches, I was able to move around a little better. She dropped me off at home and as I hobbled through the door on crutches, there was my Mama and one of our neighbors sitting there talking. They wanted to know what happened. I told them what happened and how much pain I was in, but no one suggested that I go to the hospital.

In fact, our neighbor just brushed it off and said I probably had only sprained my ankle. All I know is the pain was almost unbearable. But since Mama and our neighbor didn't seem to be overly concerned, I decided not to concern myself too much either. I figured that I would just go to sleep and when I woke up the next morning, all would be well.

That would not be the case.

I knew something was awfully wrong with my ankle when I woke up during the night to go to the bathroom. Right away, when I attempted to put my right foot on the floor, it took only a nano second to realize that I could put absolutely no pressure on that foot.

I grabbed the crutches that were conveniently propped next to my bed and used them to hobble to the bathroom. Everything was going well until the big toe of my right foot barely touched the floor. I don't even have the words to describe the pain that shot through my foot. The pain was so severe that I almost passed out. I froze in my tracks for a few moments until the pain subsided.

I finally collected myself, and made it to the bathroom, I then hobbled back to the bed knowing that the first thing on my agenda the next morning was to check myself into the emergency room. An examination of my foot was done, and x-rays were taken. It was determined that I had a torn ligament and a broken bone in my right ankle and needed surgery to repair the damage.

I was sent to the billing office to discuss how I would pay for the surgery. When I informed the billing clerk that I had no insurance and no money, she told me that I would not be able to have the surgery. When this information was relayed to the orthopedic doctor who had assessed my situation, he explained to the billing office that I needed emergency surgery and payment arrangements could be made at a later date. That was the end of that story, and before I could barely blink, an attendant showed up with a wheelchair and promptly whisked me off to the operating room.

When that orthopedic doctor said that I needed emergency surgery, he was very serious. They prepped me and had me on the operating table within the hour to perform the surgery on my right ankle. When I woke up in recovery, all I can remember is feeling as if someone was cutting my ankle with a sharp object. Of course, that is exactly what had taken place, and although the surgery was complete, I was still feeling the effects. I can recall hearing myself repeatedly say one word, and that word was "pain." I vaguely remember the nurse administering some pain medication intravenously and when I opened my eyes again, the pain had lessened.

I now had a cast on my right leg that extended from my foot up to my knee. I was told that I would have to wear that cast for a minimum of six weeks in order for my ankle to heal properly.

After being in recovery for a few hours, I was moved to a regular room and subsequently released from the hospital to begin my healing process.

I knew that my mobility would be limited because of the cast, but it never dawned on me that because of my limited mobility I would at some point be placed in harm's way when Dwight would have yet another one of his violent episodes.

The saying, *"timing is everything,"* couldn't have resonated more on what turned out to be a very eventful day.

The fact that I was partially immobilized and in the house with my brother who was prone to schizophrenic outbursts, should have reminded me to exercise caution when interacting with Dwight.

That afternoon, Dwight and I got into a heated argument about only God knows what, and I forgot who I was dealing with and my current condition.

Dwight's schizophrenia started kicking in and he didn't see a helpless person who couldn't function without the aid of crutches. I had ticked him off and he was coming for me. I braced myself emotionally and physically for what was about to happen and was hoping and praying that I would come out of the situation unharmed.

I must pause right here and give God all praises and glory because I know beyond a shadow of a doubt, that it was nobody but God who intervened at that moment.

Just as Dwight reached me to do whatever it was, he was about to do to me, which was not going to be good, my son's father miraculously showed up at our front door. He had decided to stop by to deliver a bicycle to our son. He couldn't have showed up at a better time. He quickly assessed the situation and immediately went into action.

Before Dwight could get his hands on me, my son's father managed to place himself between us. He had not only performed a tour of duty in the Navy, but he had also played football in high school. He was accustomed to running interference.

Dwight's lean one-hundred-and-sixty pound frame was no match for my son's father's solid build that was well over two-hundred pounds. As Dwight lunged for me, he was quickly subdued. Before Dwight could figure out what was happening, he was already pinned to the ground. He managed to spew out a few choice words to both of us but was otherwise incapacitated. There wasn't much more that he could do with all of that weight on top of him. Interestingly, rather than remaining combative as he had done at other times, Dwight actually calmed down very quickly.

It made me wonder if it was his mental illness operating at that moment or if it was just pure meanness that had caused Dwight to launch such an attack on me. Whatever the case, had not it been for my son's father rescuing me on that day, only God knows whether I would have survived that impending attack. Whenever Dwight snapped out, he would go in for the kill. There's no way that I would have been able to fight him off that day because I was unable to walk without the aid of crutches. I guess I could have used one of my crutches to fend him off, but that's mere speculation. When Dwight would strike, he would strike like lightening. It happens so quickly that you don't even know what hit you.

Sensing that I was still not out of danger, my son's father took me away from the situation and I ended up living with a friend of his for a little while.

I was out of harm's way for the time being.

James and Dwight were still constantly in and out of the local mental health unit and or the state hospital and Donny was still doing his usual disappearing and reappearing acts. I hate to say it, but the truth of the matter is that I loved those times when they were all gone. No one was under threat, and there was peace and quiet.

> *Sudden outbursts of anger and aggression in general are a symptom of schizophrenia, and they may not have any specific cause.*

> **Anxiety:** *Like any form of mental disorder, schizophrenia puts sufferers in many stressful and difficult situations, which are often far beyond their capability to handle.*
>
> (BRIGHTQUEST TREATMENT CENTERS)

CHAPTER 13

WHEN DEATH COMES KNOCKING

It was 1983, a year that will forever be etched in my mind. Death had already come knocking twice before at my door, but it hits different depending on who it is and the circumstances. In 1977, Mama Annie, that's what we called my grand mama, died suddenly and unexpectedly. This was the very first time in my life someone died who was very close to me. I felt like my heart had been broken into a trillion pieces when I was told the only grandparent that I ever had the privilege of knowing was gone. I remember being eight months pregnant during the time of Mama Annie's passing. That was a tough one, but over time, the pain got a little easier. Never again would I have the long visits to look forward to, the perfect fried chicken, homemade biscuits, and blueberry doobie.

Such is life. Then, less than two years later in January of 1979, my world was completely shattered. My worse fear became a reality. I always said I wanted to die before he did because I wouldn't be able to handle it if he died before me. Well, it didn't happen the way I hoped. When I got the news that Daddy had a stroke and wasn't expected to live, I immediately went into denial. My response to the one who brought me that devastating news was, "not my Daddy, you're not talking about my daddy." But Daddy did die, and I simply didn't know how to deal with it. This just could not be happening. Was I dreaming? But I wasn't dreaming. Daddy was gone. I was heartbroken at the passing of both my grandmamma and my Daddy, especially because they both left me suddenly and unexpectedly. If they had been sick, it would've still hurt, but at least I may have seen it coming. All I know is that their deaths left a hole in my heart that would not be filled soon.

Then death came to visit our family again. You might say I was somewhat prepared for this one because of the dream I'd had several days prior to this third death. But what can ever really prepare you for the death of a loved one?

I'd had dreams before that had come true, and this dream was so vivid that I silently prayed this would not be one of those dreams that would come true.

In this dream, I was in bed taking a nap and it was interrupted when someone knocked on the front door. I answered the door and our neighbor from two houses down, was standing there. When I opened the door, she informed me that someone from the Florida State Hospital had just called to inform us that my brother James was dead. At that point, I abruptly awakened from my nap in a cold sweat, and of course, I was terribly relieved when I realized I had been dreaming. It wasn't just a dream though, that was a nightmare. Even though I didn't want to entertain it, I somehow knew and feared that was one of those dreams that meant something. My concern was confirmed when in just a few days I would be shaken to the very core of my being when I would have to live out that nightmare.

That day, I woke up and decided to call off from work. I wasn't sick, I just didn't feel up to going to work that day. You might say that I was feeling melancholy. Around mid-afternoon I was in my room taking a nap and was awakened by a knock at the door. When I answered the door, our neighbor from two doors down was standing there and at that moment I experienced one of the worst feelings that I had ever felt in the pit of my stomach.

I should mention that we didn't have phone service at home at the time. We were experiencing a financial hardship and our telephone service had been temporarily suspended. Our neighbor had been gracious enough to allow us to share her phone number with some important contacts in case of an emergency. One such contact was the Florida State Hospital in Chattahoochee, Florida, where my brother James had been a patient for several months. As I stood there waiting for our neighbor to speak, I immediately had a flashback of the dream that I'd had a few days earlier and I felt weak at the knees.

I already knew or at least thought I knew what was about to come out of her mouth. You see, my interaction with her was eerily playing out just like the dream I'd had. By nature, I am a very optimistic person which made me want to believe that this conversation would go well.

I will never forget the words she said to me. Even to this day, I can see her standing there at the door and I can hear her as plainly as ever. These were her words, "Cynthia, the State Hospital is on the phone and it's about James, they need you to come to the phone." I kind of let out a sigh of relief because at least she hadn't said what I thought she would say. I thought she was going to tell me that my brother was dead. But it wasn't over just yet. That walk to her house, which was only two doors down, seemed like it took forever. That was probably because I purposely tried to make that walk last as long as possible. That was one phone call that I was absolutely sure I didn't want to take. In somewhat of a fog, my legs feeling like rubber and lead at the same time, and my heart racing almost out of control, I finally got to the neighbor's house and picked up the phone. A staff member from the hospital identified herself and then informed me that my brother was missing from the hospital.

I breathed a sigh of relief since this news was much better than what I had expected. I had expected them to tell me that my brother was dead. Missing was a lot better than dead is what I was thinking. Perhaps this time, my dream would not be accurate. She went on to explain to me the circumstances surrounding my brothers' disappearance.

My brother had what was known as "ground privileges" which allowed him the freedom to go outside the hospital for supervised outdoor activities, and this had been one of those days. It seems that on this day, the patients had ventured a little ways from the facility. I was told that when it was time for the patients to go back inside the hospital and the head count was done, it was discovered that one person was missing. Regrettably, that missing person was my brother James.

The person with whom I spoke informed me that at that time they were doing everything possible to locate my brother and that they would keep us updated. I hung up the phone, thanked my neighbor for coming to get me for the phone call, and walked back to my house basically in the same manner that I had walked to her home; in a daze, feeling completely numb, and hoping they would find my brother and he would be okay. I really didn't know what to think.

I decided not to call Mama and tell her since she was at work. Besides, there was nothing that she could do anyway. I waited for her to come home from work to tell her this unsettling news.

When Mama came home from work, I told her about the bad news that I'd gotten earlier from the state hospital, and she immediately began planning for us to visit the hospital the following day. The hospital was in

Chattahoochee, Florida, which was about two hours away. I owned a car, but it was in no condition at the time to do a road trip, so Mama called our good friend Mr. Bell and asked him if he would drive us to the hospital. He kindly agreed to do so, and we made plans to leave very early the next morning to go to Florida State Hospital to meet with the hospital administrator to discuss my brothers' disappearance. As planned, we got up early the next morning and prepared to take a trip to the hospital having no earthly idea of what we would encounter. Of course, we were hoping and praying that by the time we reached the hospital the staff would greet us with the great news that my brother had been found and was safely back on his unit.

Mr. Bell promptly pulled up as he had promised in front of our house early the next morning to pick up me and Mama in his immaculate Blue Buick Electra 225, a.k.a. Deuce and a Quarter. I don't know why, but before we hit the road, Mr. Bell got out of the driver's seat and beckoned for me to take the seat. He moved to the back seat and Mama sat up front with me.

We started our journey to the state hospital in Chattahoochee.

The mood was pretty somber in the car that morning, obviously because of the situation. Mama is usually a chatter box, but the conversation was very limited. We passed the time by listening to the gospel songs that were playing on the radio.

Mama and I had made this trip quite a few times, but never under these circumstances.

Now as you are nearing Chattahoochee, there is a very narrow bridge that you have to cross that no one was particularly fond of crossing. It could barely accommodate two opposite lanes of traffic. That day, crossing the bridge would be exceptionally challenging because I was driving this huge car. Normally I would have been driving my little AMC Hornet, which was a compact car, and even that small car could be challenging on that bridge.

Imagine me having to drive across that bridge in a car that was virtually three times the size of what I was accustomed to, it proved to be extremely nerve wracking, especially under the unpleasant circumstances.

It was beginning to make sense to me why Mr. Bell would insist that I drive to Chattahoochee. Perhaps he was not that excited about driving across that bridge either. Maybe, just maybe he had the same fear that a lot of folks had about driving across that narrow bridge. At any rate, as we were approaching the bridge, I had to take several deep breaths and concentrate on negotiating that bridge without crashing into those flimsy looking rails that were the only barrier between us and the murky waters of the Chattahoochee River.

Someway and somehow, I managed to get across that bridge without crashing into the railing.

There's a song that came on the radio during our trip that sticks out in my mind. Hearing that song just added to an already somber mood. The song says,

'I don't feel noways tired, I've come too far from where I started from, Nobody told me that the road would be easy, I don't believe He's brought me this far to leave me.'

It took everything I had to not have a meltdown while that song was playing. Although, it's a song meant to provide encouragement in tough times, it had an adverse effect on me that day. My heart was bleeding.

We finally arrived at the state hospital, and most of the details of that visit are very foggy. I can't remember who exactly it was we met with, but we were basically told the same thing we had been told when we had been contacted the day before. A group of patients had gone outside of the building that morning and when they were preparing to go back inside, and the headcount was done, they realized my brother James was missing. I hardly can recall any details about the meeting that day, but there is one detail that I do remember and that is we didn't know any more about the whereabouts of my brother when we left that hospital that day than we did when we arrived there that morning. We returned home to Panama City and just waited for news about James, hoping and praying for the best. Each day that passed yielded no news about my brothers' whereabouts; it was torture.

When James had been missing for two weeks, we finally received the shocking news. My brother's body had been discovered floating in the Chattahoochee River. Yes, the same river that we had driven over on that narrow bridge the day after James was reported missing. Imagine it being possible that we could have driven right over the spot where my brother's lifeless body was floating.

The question was, how did my brother end up in the river? According to the staff at Florida State Hospital, my brother had committed suicide. So how did they know that my brother had committed suicide? There was never any mention of a suicide note. Had my brother really committed suicide, or had he just fallen into the river? The thought of my brother climbing up on the rail of the bridge and jumping over was inconceivable. What a way to end your life.

We were told by the hospital staff that a man happened to be fishing from the bridge when this alleged incident occurred. According to this witness account, he saw a Black man leaning over the rail earlier but didn't give it much thought. He also remembered hearing a loud splash shortly thereafter but didn't link the two things. He had chalked the splashing sound up to a big fish flopping around in the water. It didn't occur to the man that the splashing sound that he heard shortly after seeing a man leaning over the rail was somehow connected until he was heard on the news one evening about a patient missing from Florida State Hospital.

Upon hearing the news, the man contacted the hospital and explained what he had witnessed the day he was on the bridge. This report prompted the authorities to begin searching the river, which subsequently led to the discovery of my brothers' body.

There's a huge "what if" that lingers in my mind and that is what if the man had seen my brother fall or jump into the river that day? Perhaps James could have been rescued and this story may have turned out differently. But such was not the case.

Once my brother's body was recovered, my family had to rely on the funeral director's word that it was in fact my brother James who had been found in the river.

The funeral director strongly recommended that we not attempt to identify the body due to the extremely decomposed state after being in the water for two weeks. He told us that he was able to make a positive identification that it was indeed my brother who had been found. His identification was based on the staff's recollection of what my brother was wearing at the time of his disappearance. I don't know how true all of that is, but oddly enough, we took everyone's word for it and never pursued the matter. I tried to convince Mama to hire a lawyer and sue the hospital for what I believe was negligence, but she refused. I regret not taking it upon myself to sue them. I was still rather young and just didn't have the wherewithal to follow up.

It's funny that for a period of time after my brother's suicide I would have recurring dreams where he was still alive. At one point I even considered that there was a possibility that my brother could very well be alive since after all, we really didn't know who or what was in that coffin on the day of his funeral. We never personally identified the body. We just accepted what the funeral director told us. I think I may have just been in denial for a while and perhaps that could have been the origin of the dreams. I finally accepted the fact that James was really gone.

Now you would think things couldn't get any worse after the devastating news of James committing suicide, oh but they did. Indeed, they did.

Psychiatric inpatients constitute a population at considerably increased risk for suicide. Identifying those at imminent risk is still a challenging task for hospital staff.

Preventive measures during hospitalization include thorough assessment of suicidal features, an emphasis on the development of future perspectives, and a review of hospital regulations for patients who want to leave the ward.

(FRONTIERS MEDIA S.A.)

CHAPTER 14

HE LOST IT

Dwight was doing much better than he had in a long time, but at the shocking news of James' death, he lost it.

Someone found Dwight pouring kerosene throughout the yard of our next-door neighbor's house and telling the person he intended to set the house on fire. Before he could get his plan into full action, the fire department was called to the scene and Dwight's plans were thwarted. Although the fire was never set, due to the amount of gasoline that had been poured in the yard, the investigators for the fire department wanted to question Dwight. When confronted about his actions, Dwight became aggressive and physically assaulted one of the investigators, giving him a black eye. He was able to be calmed down, and interestingly, he wasn't taken to the emergency room or to jail.

I don't know. Maybe it was because of the whole situation with my other brother committing suicide and Mama pleading with them not to take Dwight away. But you can best believe it would have been better if she would have let him be taken away. He calmed down for the time being, but it wasn't over just yet. As if it were not bad enough that we had to deal with the difficult task of making funeral arrangements for James, in the midst of all of that, we were constantly having to monitor Dwight's behavior, which is precisely why he needed to have been admitted to the mental health unit the day he poured gasoline in the neighbor's yard and assaulted the fire investigator. There would have been at least 72 hours of peace at our home and Dwight's medications could have been regulated so that he would have been able to cope better with the situation at hand.

I know at this point Mama's emotions were running wild as well as everyone else's, but I wish that she would have taken just a few moments to really think it through before she decided to not have Dwight taken away. He just continued to wreak havoc at every turn, and we never knew how, when, or where he would strike. There were times when we could foresee things coming with him and we were able to position ourselves to respond accordingly, but at other times he operated very covertly, and we wouldn't see things coming until it was upon us.

One of his covert moves involved some interaction with Mama's sisters. He went behind our backs and called them warning them not to show up for the funeral and threatening to kill them if they did. Because my aunts knew Dwight's history and how volatile he could become, they cancelled any plans to come and support their sister. Try not to judge me for what I'm about to say, but at that time, I felt like it served Mama right because had she allowed him to be admitted to the mental health unit several days earlier when he had become unstable, things may have been different.

Of all the years we had been dealing with my brothers' illnesses, you would have thought by this time Mama could have cared less about what anyone thought. But sad to say, after all this time, she was still wrestling with the stigma attached to mental illness. Unfortunately for her, her sisters would not physically be by her side to support her during a time when she really needed them the most.

On the same night that he attempted to start a fire at the neighbor's house and that didn't work out, Dwight decided to go on a rampage at our house. I was in my bedroom that was toward the back of the house when I caught wind of a commotion in the front part of the house. In the midst of the commotion, I overheard Dwight say, "I got one more that I got to git." I had a feeling that the one more that he was referring to was me and I could hear that he was headed in the direction of my bedroom. I had to think fast because if he cornered me in that bedroom, I would be in big trouble. As I heard him coming through the house towards my bedroom I went into a panic mode, but I had to make a quick decision. I was facing a serious dilemma for two reasons. One reason was that Dwight stood between me and any reasonable exit that could be used for my escape, and the other reason was that I believed my toddler was somewhere between me and Dwight.

In a matter of seconds, I had to convince myself that crazy or not, Dwight would never harm my child because he absolutely adored that kid. Don't judge me for what happened next, but I made the snap decision to get the hell out of dodge and trust that my son would be okay.

Incidentally, I was already in my pajamas dressed for bed but obviously, based on what I did next, what I was wearing was the very last thing on my mind. The only thing that I could see at that moment was the danger signs flashing before my eyes. I knew what Dwight was capable of and I was no match for him.

Without hesitating, I hurried over to my bedroom window, raised it up and jumped out, feeling my feet hit the ground just as I could hear Dwight bursting into my room. Our house was an older construction and set high up off the ground which meant that my bedroom window was several feet from the ground. I could have very easily been injured when I jumped out that window, but that was a chance I had to take. Fortunately, when I jumped, I landed perfectly on my feet with no injuries and started running as fast as I could into the cold night, never once looking back. I've never been much of a runner, but that night running didn't pose a problem for me, and I didn't stop until I reached my friend's house that was several blocks away.

I guess for Mama that was finally the straw that broke the camel's back. I'm assuming she dialed 911 and the paramedics came and took Dwight to the emergency room, and he was admitted to the mental health unit.

I stayed at my friend's house that night and only returned home the next day after hearing that Dwight had been admitted to the mental health unit. He was there for the required 72 hours and then released. He was a little better after getting some meds into his system, but the drama was far from over.

The day of James' funeral arrived, and it appeared as though everything was under control. Of course, me and Mama were on pins and needles because we had absolutely no idea how Dwight would cope on that day. Lord knows that was by far one of the saddest days of my life. The funeral home staff arrived to drive us to the church which was only about three blocks away. I will never forget the feeling that came over me as the car pulled up in front of the church. I was so overcome with grief and had this huge urge to just start screaming to the top of my lungs until no more sound could come from me.

It took everything that I had in me not to do it because I didn't want to upset Mama and I certainly didn't want to trigger Dwight. I simply didn't want to lose my composure like that. The funeral service was somewhat of a blur to me, and I remember very few details about it, but there's one detail that I can vividly recall. But before I mention that, let me just say that on top of everything that was going on, to make matters even worse, my brother Donny was not there. He was nowhere to be found. This was the second funeral of an immediate family member that he had missed. He wasn't at Daddy's funeral either. He was in his typical habit of just picking up and taking off and we would have no idea where he was unless he was calling or writing for money. We had tried feverishly to locate him to let him know that his brother was dead. Everything was just a mess.

At this point, I started feeling sorry for Mama because her sisters weren't able to be there to support her and she just seemed so alone. Since we weren't very close, I suppose I was not able to offer her much consolation. This was just one hell of a situation. I remember my heart just breaking as I sat there in that service staring at James' coffin. The only thing there to remind me of my brother was an eight by ten photo that set atop his coffin. I had been to many funerals in my day, but never one where the coffin had a picture resting on top of it. As far as I'm concerned, that scenario just made the whole situation pretty disturbing for me. I viewed it as morbid. Several times during the service I glanced over at my brothers' friends and could barely take watching those thirty-something years old as they fought back tears. I swear, this had to be one of the saddest situations that I had ever witnessed.

As if things were not already painful enough, to put the icing on the cake, Dwight decides to have a schizophrenic outburst. Yep, smack dab in the middle of the service, with no warning, he bolted out of his seat and literally stomped all the way down the long aisle to the front door of the church, walked out the front door and slammed it behind himself. Talk about an awkward moment. It couldn't get any more awkward than that. Everyone just stared straight ahead and pretended not to notice what had just taken place. There was just never ever an end to this madness.

I have absolutely no memory at all about what happened at the burial site.

We made it back home where during those times the repast was usually held at the home of the deceased. That's where everybody showed up to eat. The family, neighbors and friends were all there at the house. I would say about an hour or so into the repast, I noticed that the crowd suddenly began to disperse. One by one I would see individuals tiptoe over to Mama and whisper their goodbyes and then they would quietly leave. It just all seemed very strange to me that they all kind of started to leave at the same time. It was a mass exodus. What I didn't know until later is that Dwight was at it again. I can't say that I was surprised.

Someone told me, after the fact, that the reason everyone left when they did was because Dwight had been subtly approaching people and under his breathe telling them it was time to leave. Now I'm not sure what tone he used or what his exact words were to them, but whatever he said and however he said it was cause for them to immediately leave. I tell you that our house was full of folk one minute, and within a few minutes, it was totally deserted, with the exception of me, Mama, Dwight, and my son. The madness just never ever ceased.

Things seemed to calm down somewhat in the days following the funeral and it was a nice change.

Of course, I had taken bereavement leave from work for my brother's funeral. I really never went into great detail with my employer about the death in my family, except to say that my brother had passed, and I would need to take funeral leave. When I returned to work, I decided to share a few details with one of my co-workers about what had actually happened to my brother to cause his death. I also shared with her a little history about my other mentally ill brothers. When I finished telling her some of my story, she just sat there in awe, shaking her head. I will never forget the words she said to me. She said, "No one would have ever believed what you have being going through." She said, "You come to work and act as if nothing is going on." And she was right. Up to that point, I had never really discussed my brothers' issues with anyone outside of my immediate family or close friends. I guess at that time, sharing my story with someone other than family or close friends was not only sobering, but therapeutic for me.

It made me realize that this was definitely my reality, and I could choose to allow this situation to cripple me or use it as a steppingstone to make me a stronger person. I knew at that moment that I would not allow this insanity, that I was surrounded by, to cripple me. Neither would I allow it to define who I was. The word was out that all of "them" were crazy, and I was determined to prove to everyone that not all of the Mobleys were crazy.

> *If you find it difficult to come to terms with your sibling's or parent's mental illness, there are many others who share your difficulty. Most siblings and adult children of people with psychiatric disorders find that mental illness in a brother, sister, or parent is a tragic event that changes everyone's life in many basic ways. Strange, unpredictable behaviors in a loved one can be devastating, and your anxiety can be high as you struggle with each episode of illness and worry about the future. It seems impossible at first, but most siblings and adult children find that over time they do gain the knowledge and skills to cope with mental illness effectively. They do have strengths they never knew they had, and they can meet situations they never even anticipated.*
>
> (HEALTHY PLACE)

CHAPTER 15

NEW RESIDENCE— SAME DRAMA

Fast forwarding a few years ahead, Daddy was gone, James was gone, Donny was nowhere to be found, and Dwight was in the state hospital again.

Mama and I decided it was time to move. So, after spending my entire life at 1002 East 9th Court, we were moving. I was literally born in that house where I had been delivered by a mid-wife.

We moved into the Henry Kirkland Apartments, the projects. This was the first time in my life that I had ever lived in the projects. This certainly was a new experience for me.

There was only Mama, me, and my son and we were enjoying a little bit of peace. Dwight was eventually released from the state hospital and came to live with us at the apartment. If I would have had a say in the matter, he would have never come to live with us, but that was Mama's son, and she would not have it any other way. Besides, I guess he really had nowhere else to go. I was hoping that he would have consented to living in a halfway house or group home, but he just flat out refused. That was primarily because he did not want to live in a structured environment, but rather in an environment where he could just run amuck and do what he wanted to and that's exactly what he did.

In the beginning when he came home, everything was going okay, but I knew from past experience that this would not last long. I wasn't being pessimistic, but I knew the routine. The first sign that he wouldn't last very long was the mere fact that he wouldn't even consider living in a group home or halfway house. The second sign was when he started falling off the bandwagon with his follow up visits to the guidance clinic. It would be just a matter of time before the drama would begin.

Now Dwight was the type of person that if he liked you, it was all good, but if he didn't like you, he would make life as miserable as he possibly could for you.

Well, I had this one friend that he seemed to like a whole lot at first, and then things changed. The reason things changed was that my friend had a tendency toward heavy use of profanity and to Dwight that was very offensive. It was offensive to him not because of him but because of Mama.

Mama was a devout Christian and never used profanity and Dwight felt that my friend was being disrespectful to Mama. This friend would often visit us and of course she brought her mouth along with her and all of its expletives. Sad to say, even though her profanity was an offense to us, neither Mama nor I had the guts to check her on this. Mama would just complain about her foul mouth behind her back and grin in her face when she came to visit. The truth is though; Mama really liked her a lot. I just simply never said anything to her about how her profanity was offensive to all of us because I didn't want to hurt her feelings. I know. That makes a lot of sense, right? If nothing else, I learned a valuable lesson from all of this, and that lesson was not addressing an issue will not make it go away. Honestly, I don't even know if us addressing it would have made her stop cussing. After all, bad habits are hard to break. Maybe she would have really tried to stop cussing around Mama or just simply stayed away.

At any rate, it was never addressed, and she continued to come over and she continued to cuss. It got to the point that when she would come over, Dwight would become very agitated, pacing back and forth, and murmuring under his breath. What was interesting about the whole situation is that his murmurings would be directed toward her, and she didn't have a clue. She would continually address Dwight throughout her conversation. He would respond to her, but at the same time he would still be very upset with her. This went on for a while and I could tell that Dwight was starting to reach a boiling point. What I started doing when she would show up at our house, was always to find a reason to hurry up and leave.

One day she finally got it that Dwight was very unhappy with her even though she didn't know why. She was visiting that day having driven over in her brand spanking new car. As usual, she was doing her normal cussing but that day, Dwight was just not having it. We noticed that Dwight went into the kitchen and took something from the refrigerator and then went outside. He was acting very suspicious. We really didn't think much of his actions until he came back inside with a big smirk on his face and went to his room. He was unusually quiet during the remainder of my friend's visit.

My friend finally decided to leave and once we went outside to her car, everything immediately made sense. We then realized what Dwight had taken from the refrigerator and why he had come back inside with that smug look on his face. He had taken raw eggs from the refrigerator and smashed them on my friend's car. If you don't already know, then let me tell you that raw eggs can cause almost irreversible damage to the paint job on a car if not dealt with immediately. When we walked out to that parking lot and saw the eggs smashed on my friend's car, we were utterly speechless. Thank God we discovered the results of Dwight's mischievous act when we did because the eggs had not stayed on the car long enough to cause any damage to her paint job. I shudder to think what the aftermath would have looked like and what her response would have been if things had turned out differently. Needless to say, after that incident, she stopped coming over.

We talked about the incident afterwards and she would always ask the question why he would do something like that? She knew that he was mentally ill, but it still needed to make sense to her why he had chosen to do that. After all, she believed he really liked her, so this was very puzzling for her. Well of course, I knew why Dwight had done what he did, but I never told her.

Yes, we were at a new residence, but the drama remained the same. It just became totally unbearable to live there and you're probably wondering why I continued to do so. Well, Mama and I had initially gotten the apartment together and it was supposed to be just the two us and my son. It seemed that the last time that Dwight was committed to the state hospital that he would be there for quite some time. As things would have it, it didn't work out that way and he was released much sooner than expected. Because he refused to live in a halfway house or group home, he would have been left homeless. So of course, Mama wouldn't have her child become homeless. I was upset that he was coming to live with us, but I couldn't be very upset with her. I only say that because I suppose that if I were in Dwight's shoes, I would've wanted Mama to have the same consideration for me.

It's just that what made this situation so unique was the fact that Dwight's mental illness, which he chose not to manage made life extremely difficult for us. Sadly, those in his immediate space were subject to his wrath when he wasn't maintaining his treatment plan, which was most of the time. I chose to remain there for the time because his release from the state hospital had caught us completely off guard and I was not in a position at that time to move away.

I did finally move away but not before witnessing him flip out just one last time before I moved.

Dwight probably had been off his medication for some time, and he was starting to get out of hand.

He was out of control again. But for the grace of God, Mama could have been seriously injured or dead that day. I can't remember what triggered him this time, but all I remember is that during his uncontrollable rage, he grabbed a cast iron skillet and hit Mama in her head with it. Like I said, it was only God's grace that saved her because to this day, I cannot understand how this tiny little woman was able to withstand that blow. To my recollection, she never even faltered when he struck her, and I don't even recall her having a knot on her head. It was truly a miracle.

Dwight immediately retreated to his room and was quiet. I called 911. The police came and I told them what happened. I told them where Dwight was, and they went to his room and asked him to come with them. He surprisingly complied. As they were escorting him out of the apartment, I was sitting in a chair next to the front door and when he approached me, he raised his hand as if he was about to strike me on the head.

Amazingly, it was as if some invisible force suspended his arm in mid-air because he was never able to lower his arm to execute the intended blow upon my head. The police peaceably escorted him outside, but when they attempted to place him in the police cruiser, a struggle ensued. Dwight was refusing to get into the car. The cops eventually overpowered him, and he was secured in the car and taken away.

Dwight ended up in the state hospital once again, but by the time he would be released, I would no longer be living there with Mama…thank

God. While Dwight was hospitalized, I met someone, fell in love, and got married. Even though I was twenty-five years old, you might say that I was marrying to get away from home. My knight in shining armor had arrived and would take me away from all of the pandemonium.

Why follow-up appointments are important for mental health?

A follow-up visit is important because: good follow-up care helps lower the risk of repeat trips to the hospital. You may need extra support right after leaving the hospital. If you're on medication, it allows your doctor to evaluate and adjust your medication.

(MANAGED HEALTH NETWORK)

CHAPTER 16

HERE WE GO AGAIN

Life was relatively calm for a while and then Dwight was once again released from the hospital. Things didn't appear to be so bad because finally, it was only him living with Mama, just the way he liked it. He, being the only one living with her suited him just fine because he could pretty much do what he wanted to do without being held accountable. He basically was controlling Mama. I'm one hundred percent sure that he was causing turmoil over there, but she just wasn't telling.

Dwight knew that I had gotten married, but he had not yet met my husband. When Dwight first met my husband, he seemed to like him okay and they got along just fine. I don't know what caused it, but at some point, things changed, and Dwight stopped liking him. And then the craziness started happening again; this time involving my new husband.

I had already explained to him that Dwight had mental problems, so he wasn't surprised when Dwight started acting out.

The episode that sticks out in my mind, and yes, I did say episode, because it was a continuation of the madness that just seemed to never go away.

My husband and I were visiting Mama's apartment one day and the three of us began to notice that Dwight's behavior was becoming increasingly suspicious. He just looked like he was up to no good. I finally just ignored him, but I couldn't help but notice that my husband wasn't ignoring him. I'm not sure what prompted it, but the two of them at first got into a verbal argument and things quickly took a turn for the worse.

My husband had figured out that Dwight was plotting to damage his car. What was the deal with Dwight and folks' cars? And didn't he know that there are two things that you don't mess with that belong to a man? His woman or his car.

At that point, little did Dwight know that he was plunging into something that he was going to have to fight his way out of, literally. This fight would be like no other that he had encountered, because unlike the cops and all of the others, we would soon find out that my husband would have no mercy on Dwight.

The verbal exchange continued for just a few moments and ended with my husband saying to Dwight in a threatening tone that he had better not be thinking about doing anything to his car. Dwight's response to him was a notable snicker that sort of confirmed his plans. That statement to him actually seemed to be just the push that he needed to go ahead and execute his diabolical plan. Dwight started for the front door with my husband right on his heels.

As they both went out the front door, me and Mama knew that this situation was not going to be pretty. Mama and I watched from the living room window as Dwight began circling the car like a vulture circling a dead carcass and my husband was still right on his heels and telling him what he was going to do to him if he touched his car. Now mind you they were both about equal in height, but their body composition was quite different. Dwight was rather thin with no obvious muscle, and my husband, on the other hand, was quite muscular. It appeared that at some point, partial sanity returned to Dwight because it seemed as though he suddenly realized that he needed to move away from the car. He started heading back to the front door of the apartment with my husband still right on his heels as they continued to exchange words.

You would have thought that after Dwight moved away from the car that my husband would have relaxed, but by this time the verbal altercation was becoming more intense. He not only followed Dwight into the house but into his bedroom and that's when *all hell broke loose*. The verbal altercation turned into a physical altercation and as badly as Mama and I were wishing that he would have been a little more understanding with regards to the fact that my brother's mental illness was mostly responsible for all of this, my husband wasn't in the least bit understanding. His anger had really kicked in by now and he was going in for the kill.

I can still hear the sound, even as I'm writing this, of his fists pounding my brother's body. He had Dwight pinned to the bed and was beating him like there would be no tomorrow. Now here was the spooky part about this whole situation. As he continued pummeling Dwight like he was a punching bag, Dwight just laid there laughing hysterically and taking the blows. Every time he punched Dwight, he just laughed harder. Dwight acted like he was getting some type of a high from the punching. I think that was the insanity kicking in even more.

Dwight finally wriggled himself from underneath the clutches of his aggressor and ran into the bathroom. Everybody breathed a sigh of relief thinking that it was over until all of a sudden Dwight came rushing out of the bathroom carrying an open bottle of rubbing alcohol in his hand and before anybody could figure out what was happening, he hurled the alcohol directly into my husband's face.

You can imagine the shock factor of all of us when that happened. Becoming more infuriated by this treacherous act, my husband commenced to landing a few more blows to Dwight before the pain of the rubbing alcohol, which had actually penetrated one of his eyes, took over. My husband was unable to fight anymore because of the alcohol that was in his eye and Dwight decided to retreat to his bedroom. My husband left him alone because he was feeling the full effect of the alcohol in his eye.

We rushed out to take him to the emergency room so he could have the rubbing alcohol flushed from his eye. Fortunately for him, there hadn't been any permanent damage. That day, we decided that we wouldn't visit Mama for a while so Dwight could have an opportunity to calm down.

It wasn't long after the altercation between the two of them that Dwight went off the deep end in public and did something that ultimately ended with him back in the state hospital. Once again, we could be at peace. It was such a great feeling when we could go about our daily lives and not have to worry about being in the middle of any type of confusion, although we knew that it would always be just a matter of time before Dwight would be released from the state hospital again. Sadly, we could never totally exhale because we just never knew when we would get the call that he was being released. In the meantime, we just had to go on with our lives.

One of the symptoms of schizophrenia is hallucinations: The person may see, hear, taste, smell, or feel things that are not real. The most common form of hallucinations are auditory, and they include hearing voices that nobody else can hear, even when no one is around, says Dr. D'Souza. The voices may be friendly, threatening, abusive, critical, or annoying. They may talk to the person, have discussions with them, or give them instructions. Hallucinations can be very real to the person experiencing them.

(VERYWELLMIND)

CHAPTER 17

HE POPPED UP AND POPPED OUT

Our peaceful periods were always short-lived.

It was unbelievable how we seemed to continually live in this vicious cycle.

Dwight was in the state hospital again, and then my brother Donny pops up. Remember, Donny is my brother who disappears and reappears in and out of town at will. Mind you, Donny had been missing for a few years and I have to admit that I have only myself to thank for his resurfacing.

As hellacious as things could be when they were around, after all, these were still my brothers and I loved them. I had already lost my oldest brother to suicide, and I didn't want anything bad to happen to the remaining two. Yes, I wanted them out of my hair because of the threats that were imposed when their minds would snap, especially Dwight, but I certainly didn't want them dead. Locked away maybe, but not dead. I could deal with them being institutionalized, because at least they were getting help, and everyone was out of harm's way for the most part.

Unlike Dwight, Donny never acted in a way to pose a threat to anyone or himself. Maybe that's why he had avoided being institutionalized. His behavior was of another breed. As I started to say earlier, I have no one but myself to thank for Donny's resurfacing. After he had been missing for an exceptionally long period of time, I became concerned that my brother may have been in trouble. With this thought heavy on my heart, I shared my concerns with my church family and during one of our services; we prayed that my brother would return home. There's a saying that you should be careful what you pray for because you just might get it. I discovered, in this case, that there was a lot of truth to that statement.

It could not have been more than a week or two that my brother showed up after our church congregation had prayed for his return. Needless to say, I was as happy as a lark when my long, lost brother returned home, but that happiness was temporary.

My doorbell rang one day and when I opened the door, there stood Donny.

To this day, I have no idea how Donny knew where me and my new husband lived.

I had never been so glad in my life to see my brother. I grabbed him and hugged him as tightly as I could, not noticing at the time, his blank expression. I knew that my brother was suffering from mental illness, but it had been so long since I had seen him that I wasn't thinking about that at the time. After I had calmed down a bit, reality set in, and I remembered that my brother was suffering from mental illness. It didn't matter. My brother was finally home again, and I was overjoyed to see him. I showed him to his room where he could put his things down and freshen up a bit and then I fixed him something to eat.

Donny had been there for just a short while when I started to notice an unusual odor. It's funny that I hadn't noticed it before, but I guess I had been distracted by the excitement of seeing him after such a long time. I determined that the terrible odor was coming from his body. It seems like the longer he stayed, the more intense the odor became.

It was so bad that I could barely catch my breath at times. It hadn't dawned on me that my brother had probably been sleeping on the streets and God only knows when the last time was that he'd had a good hot shower or bath. Well, he was home now, and we would get that taken care of. That was an easy fix. Or so I thought. Well, it proved not to be such an easy fix after all. He just flat out refused to go anywhere near soap and water. At the time, we lived in a two- bedroom townhouse and I allowed Donny to share my son's bedroom.

My son probably resents me to this day for putting him through this traumatic ordeal. It was a relatively small bedroom, and it didn't take long for the stench to settle in. No amount of air freshener that we used could alleviate the smell, so we just had to deal with it. He basically never left the room except to eat and go to the bathroom and he didn't talk to anyone. It was the oddest situation ever. My husband, thank God, was very kind and was very tolerant of the situation, and we managed to hang in there.

The once joyous homecoming celebration of Donny had turned into something totally different. We tried our best to treat him as normal as possible, but how do you treat an abnormal person normal? We pretty much started just trying to keep our distance and left him to himself. Approximately a week passed and one day when I came home from work, Donny was gone.

As happy as I was to see my brother show up at my doorstep a week earlier, I was equally as happy when I came home and found him gone again. In retrospect, I regret that we didn't do more to help him; like trying to get him into some type of treatment. Then I vaguely recall that we did try, but he wasn't cooperative.

Although I was happy that he left again because of the awkwardness of the situation, today I'd give anything to see my brother pop up just one more time.

There is clearly a link between psychiatric disorders and homelessness; disentangling the nature of this relationship is complicated. Regardless of mental health status, people who are homeless generally have a history marked by poverty and social disadvantage, including considerable poverty in childhood and lower levels of education, and they are likely to belong to an ethnic minority. Mental illness had preceded homelessness in about two-thirds of the cases.

(PSYCHIATRIC TIMES)

CHAPTER 18

HIS LAST HOORAH

Since Donny had chosen to remain out of sight for the time being and my brother James had died, that left only Dwight to contend with, and he was a handful.

He had done another stint in the state hospital and had once again been released. By this time, I'd lost count of how many times Dwight had been in and out of the state hospital. He would end up in the state hospital one last time and this time it would become his permanent home.

I showed up to work one day for my 7:30 a.m. shift, as a registrar in the emergency room of one of the local hospitals. As I completed charting from the previous shift, I noticed that my brother Dwight had been admitted to the emergency room on the two previous shifts. I really thought that in times past things had been really bad for Dwight, but this was an indication that things were definitely going from bad to worse for him. To be checked into the emergency room twice in less than 24 hours was a bit extreme. Interestingly enough, each time he had been released from the emergency room right back onto the streets.

It makes you wonder what was going on in the minds of the hospital staff. Sadly, it appears as though they had grown accustomed to seeing Dwight in the emergency room, and I guess they just felt as though there was nothing else, they could do for him. So, this time, he didn't even get admitted to the mental health unit. They just discharged him back to the streets and he went out there and acted out and ended up right back at the emergency room.

My brother's final visit to the emergency room just so happened to be during my shift. It was at the end of my shift when the police walked through the door with my brother in handcuffs and escorted him to the registration desk where I sat. I was embarrassed and hurt at the same time. I was embarrassed, of course, because this was my brother presenting to the emergency room with mental health issues during my shift. Most of my coworkers knew who he was and knew about his situation, but to have things go down this way was not my ideal situation, but I managed to deal with it.

I was more hurt, though, than embarrassed because of my brother's appearance. He looked like he had been run over by a train. He had been beaten up pretty badly by the police. One of Dwight's eyes was black, and he told me right in front of the police officer that another police officer, yes the one who had sworn to protect and serve, was the one who had given him the black eye. This was not confirmed by anyone else, but I believed my brother.

One of the officers that was accompanying Dwight did tell me that Dwight was claiming that he was HIV positive and had spit on one of the officers. If this, in fact, did happen, then that was probably the officer that had given him the black eye. I guess I should thank God that they didn't kill him, even though from the looks of him, they surely tried. I remember him being released from the emergency room that day back into the custody of the police. Apparently, there must have been some type of crime committed, but I was not aware of the charges. The next time we heard from Dwight, he had once again been admitted to the state hospital. This time he would remain there for a very long time.

Since 2015, nearly a quarter of all people killed by police officers in America have had a known mental illness. Injuries, too, are common although they are less carefully tracked. (NPR)

As of July 16, 2022, all calls and text messages to "988" route to a 988 Suicide and Crisis Lifeline call center. The 988 Suicide and Crisis Lifeline provides 24/7, confidential support to people in suicidal crisis or mental health-related distress.

Nationwide, communities are starting to build comprehensive and coordinated crisis systems to improve responses to people experiencing a behavioral health crisis and reduce overreliance on law enforcement officers in these situations. Typically, crisis responses originate from people calling the general 911 emergency line for help. However, this is an inefficient way to connect people to immediate behavioral health services, as it overburdens the 911 system and may introduce law enforcement to situations that do not require a police response. In 2020, the Federal Communications Commission (FCC) and Congress established a universal phone number for mental health crises and suicide.

CHAPTER 19

THE STATE HOSPITAL

We would make frequent visits to the state hospital to see Dwight and they were usually quite interesting. One reason is because it seems like he was hardly ever in the same place and that was because of his constant noncompliant behavior. Dwight's inpatient status was mentally ill with criminal charges. Therefore, he was confined in the Forensic Unit. I absolutely hated going to that place because trying to locate my brother was extremely complicated and frustrating to say the least.

We would usually stop at the main building to determine where he was housed. I can't remember even one time when we were directed to him, and he was actually where they said he was. Most of the time, it took us two or three tries before we would actually locate him. I don't know if we were just stupid and couldn't follow directions or if they were just that unorganized. Maybe, a little bit of both.

I remember one time driving to so many buildings at that facility that I was simply ready to turn around and go back home. The way the place was laid out was totally confusing. It was especially confusing when Dwight would be housed in solitary confinement because that building was quite a distance from the other buildings, and that campus was a maze.

We would usually spend so much time trying to locate him that by the time we found him, we only had a very short time to visit him.

This wasn't a problem for me at all, but it was for Mama. For me, the shorter the visit, the better. Even locked up, he was still quite dramatic, and I was never really up to dealing with him.

Most of the time, once we would locate the building, parking close by was an issue. We would have to walk what seemed like a mile to the actual building. Then once in the building, we would have to be cleared through security which was a tedious task. Once cleared through security, we would have to wait for what seemed like an eternity for the staff to bring him out. Because just as visitors had to follow certain protocol for entrance, the patients also had certain protocol for leaving their units.

Our visits would be to a generally populated area which consisted of a few tables and chairs.

There were vending machines located in the area and the first thing Dwight wanted to know after saying hello was if Mama had change for the drink machine so he could buy Coke. He would literally drink four to five cans of Coca Cola while we visited him, lining up the empty cans on the table where we sat.

When he wasn't asking for money to buy Coke, he was usually rambling and being delusional. This type of rambling annoyed Mama and she would just keep asking him to stop talking that way. She annoyed me because she was still in denial about him being mentally ill. There we were visiting him in a mental institution, and she was insisting that he hold a conversation like a sane person.

If it weren't for the fact that I would have to hear her mouth about it, I would have gladly just dropped her off for her visit with him and waited elsewhere until she was done. I was always ready to leave as soon as he came out. I really loved my brother, but my tolerance level was at zero. I guess during those times, you might say that I had absolutely no compassion. I lacked education about mental illness which partially contributed to my reaction to him. Not to mention all the turmoil with Dwight when he was at home, which had left a seriously bad taste in my mouth. I really would try to engage him in conversation, but it was totally useless. His subject matter was of absolutely no interest to me.

There were times when he would get so carried away with his delusions and his ramblings that Mama would just sit there and roll her eyes at him. You could tell that she was beyond frustrated. He would say something like, "Well, tomorrow is the day that I brush my teeth because I only brush them every other day." She would just cringe, and I would crack up laughing. Actually, when he would say stuff like that, I'd get a kick out of watching how annoyed she became.

The best part of the visit for me was when it was time to go. Dwight would repeatedly say thanks to us for coming to visit, we'd hug and kiss and off we went. He would say bye while waving to us until he was out of sight.

Mama and I would usually argue in the car on the way back home because she insisted that he was simply acting out. I suppose that could've been partially true. It was just so hard to believe that after all of these years that she truly was still in denial. We argued because I was trying to convince her to face reality and she just absolutely refused. She would often say that there was nothing wrong with Dwight. He was just "cutting the fool," she said.

Believe it or not, the drama didn't stop because Dwight was in the state hospital. It just became a new and different type of drama.

Mama would receive in the mail several times a month a copy of a court injunction. The hospital would initiate these injunctions in order to force Dwight to take his medications which he regularly refused. Dwight was still creating drama in the state hospital and every time Mama would receive this paperwork, it just caused her to worry more than she already did about Dwight. Not only was he creating drama in that regard, but he seemed to have a permanent attachment to the telephone.

In the beginning after being admitted, he would call Mama three or four times a month. Then the phone calls started becoming more frequent. Eventually, he was calling Mama sometimes two to three times a day. Those were collect calls, so Mama was footing the bill. She would complain to me about the excessive phone calls, so I suggested to her that she set boundaries with Dwight about how often he could call. I told her that she could give him a limit on how many calls he could make to her a month.

Well, I was just wasting my breath because that didn't go over too well with her. She immediately rejected my suggestion saying that she didn't want to limit his phone calls because she would feel guilty if she didn't take his calls and then something bad happened to him. I then told her that since she wasn't open to my suggestion that I would appreciate it if she didn't complain to me anymore about the situation.

That made her angry with me, but I didn't care. I didn't get it then, but I get it now. Mama was being so accommodating to Dwight because she had already lost one son who was "in the care" of the Florida State Hospital, and she was willing to do anything within her power to make sure she didn't lose another son. Mama continued to accept the many phone calls from Dwight every day, several times a day, and she continued to complain.

I wouldn't necessarily label this next thing as drama, but I will call it very strange behavior. Dwight was a letter writer, and he wrote to Mama several times a month. Sometimes his writing was coherent and sometimes it wasn't. Sometimes it was a combination. He not only sent her letters, by the way, but she always received a card on her birthday and a greeting card on every holiday.

Dwight started this strange habit of sending Mama correspondence that contained not a letter, but shredded paper. The first time this happened she assumed that this was some sort of mistake, but she soon realized that it was not a mistake because after that, several times a week she would receive these envelopes addressed to her that contained only shredded paper. She would sometimes receive more than one at a time. We never figured out what that was all about and yes, she kept every single one of them.

A mental hospital, also known as a psychiatric hospital, is a facility that provides specialized inpatient care for mental health conditions.

Mental hospitals often provide care and treatment for people with serious mental health illnesses.

According to the National Institute of Mental Health, a serious mental illness is a mental, emotional, or behavioral condition leading to substantial impairment in a person's ability to function in their daily life and activities.

This may include major depressive disorder, schizophrenia, bipolar disorder, obsessive-compulsive disorder (OCD), and post-traumatic stress disorder (PTSD).

(VERYWELLMIND)

CHAPTER 20

AND THE DRAMA CONTINUES

I moved from Florida to Pittsburgh in February of 1996. A few months later I made a trip back home to attend my son's high school graduation ceremony. I decided to incorporate within my trip a visit to the state hospital to see Dwight. Although I hadn't seen him since leaving Florida, we often spoke on the phone. In one of our conversations, I had informed Dwight that I would be coming to Florida and was planning on visiting him. Since it had been some time since we had seen each other, we were both very excited about the visit.

I planned to fly into Tallahassee, Florida and then rent a car to drive to Panama City. My rationale was that by flying into Tallahassee, I would be close to the state hospital and could stop in for my visit with Dwight on the way to Panama City since the hospital was between Tallahassee and Panama City. So that is exactly what I did. As usual, Dwight was not in the same area of the hospital that he was in when I last visited him.

He was actually in what was called "down the hill." In other words, he had been a bad boy and had to be moved to a different unit. Down the hill was a bit of ways off from the main hospital grounds, but I eventually was able to locate the building. After finding parking, I went into the building to begin the security process. I pressed the buzzer at the security gate. When the guard answered I gave him my name and told him who I was there to see.

You could have knocked me over with a feather when I received the guards' reply that Dwight was sending a message to me that he would not be visiting with me. I could not believe my ears. I stood there for a few moments thinking that Dwight might change his mind, but he didn't. I finally accepted the fact that he wasn't going to come out to see me.

Disappointed that I couldn't see my brother, and feeling somewhat rejected, I left the building and made my way back to my car and continued my drive to Panama City. I'm sure that you've clearly seen by now that with Dwight, there was never a dull moment. I suppose he could be dubbed the king of drama. Fortunately for me, his refusing to see me didn't throw me too far off my game.

I'm glad I planned my trip the way that I did. Had I driven from Panama City to Chattahoochee to visit Dwight and he refused to see me, my reaction might have been quite different. I enjoyed my visit to Panama City and returned back to Pittsburgh a week later. I had a fleeting thought to stop past the hospital on my way back to Tallahassee, but quickly dismissed that thought. For one, I didn't want to risk missing my flight in case I arrived at the hospital and encountered the usual challenge of locating Dwight, neither did I want to show up at the hospital and have Dwight refuse my visit.

A few days after arriving back in Pittsburgh I received a call from guess who. Yes, you guessed it right. Dwight was calling me. As soon as I answered the phone, he immediately began apologizing to me for having me come to see him and he refusing to accept my visit. Of course, I had a few choice words to say to him before I accepted his apology.

After I accepted his apology, what came out of his mouth next was enough to make me want to take back accepting his apology, but I just let it go. He told me that the reason why he had refused to visit with me that day was because I had shown up during the time that his favorite soap opera was on. I waited for a few seconds for him to tell me that he was only kidding. He didn't say that he was. At that point I just considered the source and moved on to the next thing. It wasn't because I was upset with him or anything like that, but after that conversation, for whatever reason, Dwight and I did not make contact for a while. Mama kept me updated as to what was happening with him and that was good enough for me.

As it was my custom, I returned home to Panama City for a visit at least once or twice a year. Normally these visits would last about a week and usually I would crash at Mama's apartment. Since she had only one bedroom, I would usually sleep on the sofa in the living room.

It was time for a visit, so I boarded a plane and arrived safely in Panama City for a visit that I would not soon forget.

During my visit, my brother Donny who we had not seen in a while, "popped up." There was this funny thing about him. I swear he had detective abilities. He always had a way of finding folk, even if they had moved. Interestingly, no one could keep track of him, but he could certainly keep track of everyone else.

Mind you since the last time we saw Donny, Mama had moved, but that didn't stop him from finding her. I guess since Panama City is such a small town, it wouldn't be that hard. Anyway, Donny pops up and this time, he came with drama. I can't figure out for the life of me if and when he slept because I never saw him sleeping.

Listen to this bizarre behavior he was displaying during my visit. Oh, before I tell you about that, let me just give you a scenario of the living conditions. As I said, Mama had a one-bedroom apartment and there were three of us there at the time. That may not have been such a big deal because for as long as I can remember, Mama really never went to bed at night. She would sit up in a chair nodding in and out all night long and then get up about five o'clock in the morning and get in the bed, only to get up again around seven to start her day. I know, weird right? I was sleeping on the sofa, Mama sat nodding in the chair, and Donny was parked in the dining room. Now comes the crazy part. This joker would sit up all night long listening to some deceased preacher on the radio, but his sermons were still being aired. If that's what Donny wanted to do, then that was okay by me. But herein lies the problem, he would turn the volume all the way up to maximum capacity and this dead preacher's voice would be blaring through that small apartment all night long.

Mama would beg him to turn the volume down, but he just flat out refused. I was on vacation and that's what I was having to deal with. He did this foolishness every night. I know you're probably asking why I didn't get a hotel room or just go and stay with someone else. Neither of those were an option so I was stuck. Every single night for a solid week, I had to endure this madness. Now the plot thickens, and it gets weirder. Donny clearly had contempt for Mama because he was totally defiant when she would ask him to turn the volume down on that radio at night. I never addressed him because I had no idea how he would respond, and I wanted to make it back to Pittsburgh in one piece. I'm surprised no one called the police for disturbance of the peace. I wish someone had.

Now there was something that happened every day that was very peculiar and I'm not quite sure what it all meant. The moment Mama left the house to go to work, Donny would become as quiet as a mouse. As small as that apartment was, he managed to keep out of my sight. He scared the living daylights out of me once when I walked past one of his hiding places. I guess I must have startled him, and he darted past me like a scared rabbit. I guess you could say that we frightened each other. As long as it was only, he and I in that apartment, he remained hidden and silent.

I kid you not; as soon as Mama would return from work, he would reappear and start his foolishness. He generally didn't listen to the radio before nighttime. That was reserved for the wee hours of the morning. His evening routine was to just sit there in a corner in the dining room and have a conversation with himself. Mama would just get on my last nerve when she would keep trying to have a normal conversation with him. When it came to my brothers' mental illnesses, denial was Mama's order of the day, and in this case, she would tolerate anything because she was just happy that her long lost son was home—at least for the time being. I wish she would've thrown him out on his head, but of course, she wasn't about to do that.

Please don't judge me, but during that time, I didn't have one iota of compassion for him. He was screwing up my visit and I wanted to be rid of him. I finally got my wish, but boy if I could take it back!

I returned to Pittsburgh and left him there with Mama and that's the last time I saw him. When I talked to Mama sometime later, she said that he had left once again, but this time it was different. Remember I said earlier that his modus operandi would be to leave when no one was around. Mama said this time when he left, he actually let her watch him leave. When she realized that he was leaving, he was already outside walking away from her apartment. She told me that she continually called out his name, but he never looked back. That was very strange and that's the last time that she saw him. That was the last time Mama saw him, but he did show up at my aunt's home a couple of years later. My aunt lived in Leesburg, Florida and he appeared on her doorstep one day.

This is the story that my aunt told me. She said that Donny showed up at her house one day and she graciously welcomed him in. She said he stayed with her for about two months and then she told me that she just couldn't do it anymore—he just had to go. I never asked and she never told me any specifics, she just said that he couldn't stay with her any longer.

Now this next part of her story gets kind of crazy, and she really could have kept this to herself, but I'll just chalk it up to ignorance. She told me that once Donny had left her house that the police showed up at her door one day and asked her if it was her nephew who was sleeping under the bridge. Apparently, someone had previously informed her of this, and she confirmed to the police that it was indeed her nephew. My aunt told me the police told her that he really should not be sleeping under the bridge because that area was very dangerous due to being heavily populated with alligators. I suppose at that point she felt there wasn't much she could do or wanted to do, so she just did nothing. Now this was the part of the story I really wish she would've kept to herself. She told me she really believed that Donny had been eaten by an alligator. She said she was told he was last seen heading up the highway where gators frequently hung out.

And this is the part that got to me. Supposedly, and don't ask me why, a dead alligator had been found and cut opened and a white pair of sneakers were found in the gator. My aunt said she remembered Donny owning a white pair of tennis shoes and so what she was implying was that since these tennis shoes were found in this gator, he had been eaten by the gator. My problem with her story is, why would anyone be cutting open a dead alligator and if my brother had been eaten by a gator then wouldn't there be other evidence inside of the gator? Surely if those were his tennis shoes, then I would think that some body parts would have been found inside the gator as well. It just seems awfully far-fetched to me.

Well, as the years passed, it looked like Donny had just disappeared from the face of the earth. I did go so far as to do a people search on him and at the time, his trail stopped in the area of Leesburg. I really don't want to believe that my brother was eaten by an alligator, and I wish my aunt had never planted that idea in my head.

For the first time in a very long time, no one had seen or heard from Donny. It's been over two decades now, and I regularly pray for my brother and my prayer is that he is somewhere safe and sound and someday soon he will once again show up on somebody's doorstep.

Siblings of an individual with a mental illness can experience a wide range of emotions such as confusion, anger, hopelessness, and grief. This can especially be true if the person takes a supportive and/or care giving role.

They can also experience frustration with things like the mental health system, as it can feel overwhelming to understand. They can mourn their sibling in terms of "what could have been," as they might have imagined the future of their family to be quite different.

(AMI—Quebec)

CHAPTER 21

JUST ME AND DWIGHT

It was in 2002 when Mama began experiencing dementia and was later diagnosed with Alzheimer's. I moved her from Florida to live with me in Pittsburgh, and she was there until she passed away in 2011.

From the day that I told Dwight that Mama was suffering from Alzheimer's to the day she died, he refused to accept it. Or at least that's what he led me to believe. I found it ironic that Mama had remained in denial for so many years about Dwight's mental illness and now Dwight was now in denial about Mama having Alzheimer's.

Once she was living with me, she still spoke to Dwight on a regular basis, but the phone calls became few and far between once her condition began deteriorating. The calls eventually stopped altogether. Dwight was no longer sending Mama the envelopes filled with shredded paper; however, he did continue sending her cards for her birthday and holiday greeting cards. I would always read the cards to her, and she would respond with a nod or a smile.

Even though I repeatedly explained to Dwight that Mama was just "not there" anymore, and she didn't understand about the cards, he insisted on sending them anyway. When I realized that I wasn't getting through to him, I finally stopped trying to explain and just let him keep sending the cards. Sometimes I would read them to her and sometimes I wouldn't.

Mama came to live with me in 2002 and then Dwight made a transition in 2005. I received notification that he had been transferred from the Florida State Hospital to a maximum-security facility for the criminally insane in Gainesville, Florida. Also, at that time, due to Mama's condition, I became the contact person for Dwight.

Once he was transferred to this new facility, he was not able to contact us as often as he had when he was in the state hospital. This was probably for the better since Mama's condition had worsened to the point where she wouldn't even recognize who she was talking to anyway.

Not only did Dwight seem to be in denial about Mama's illness, but when she passed away, he remained in denial about her death. He just never talked about her anymore.

One day it occurred to me that although he had refused to acknowledge her illness when she was still alive, and then her death, he knew.

He knew because he eventually stopped sending the cards.

I remember a strange event that occurred when Mama passed away.

I hadn't seen Dwight in more than two decades and then Mama passed away in 2011. When I shared the sad news with Dwight, he said he wanted to come to her service. I was really looking forward to seeing Dwight. He would be traveling from Gainesville to Panama City in Florida.

So, on the day of Mama's service, we were on our way to the church when Dwight called. He said he was on 11th Street, (the street the church was on). He wanted to know the address of the church. I gave him the address and couldn't wait to see my brother Dwight.

When I arrived at the church, I was looking to spot some type of official looking vehicle that would be an indication that Dwight was there. I saw no such vehicle and figured that he would arrive shortly since when he had called me, he said that he was on eleventh street near where the church was located. I greeted relatives as they drove into the parking lot of the church, but I was slightly preoccupied because I really was looking for Dwight to show up. I waited in the parking lot of the church for quite some time for him to show up and when he didn't come, I went inside the church. Even though there was still a little time before the service would begin, I was now becoming a little concerned because Dwight still had not shown up. What was taking so long?

The service began and as it progressed, I continued to look for Dwight, even commenting during the service a few times that I was waiting for my brother to arrive. Every time the church door opened; I just knew that it would be Dwight coming through those doors. The service ended and still, no Dwight. I was sorry that he had missed the service, but I was still looking forward to seeing him and was wondering why he hadn't made it. I concluded that given his history that he'd probably changed his mind at the last minute about attending the service and was in the parking lot of the church waiting for us to come out.

After greeting everyone at the close of the service, I rushed out of the church because I just couldn't wait to see my brother. Much to my disappointment there was no Dwight in the parking lot. Now I was really concerned, but because of all that was transpiring with the service just ending and being bombarded by relatives and friends, I put this to the back of my mind temporarily.

Yes, I was a bit concerned, but I knew my brother. It wouldn't be a big surprise that, he had changed his mind about coming to the service and that the staff had just turned around and driven him right back to Gainesville.

I would follow up with him when I returned to Pittsburgh. The service was held on Saturday, and I would be returning to Pittsburgh on

Monday. When I got back to Pittsburgh, I called the facility where Dwight was housed to find out why Dwight never showed up at the church that day. I was not prepared for the answer that I would receive. Dwight's counselor, Charlie, with whom I had a great rapport, chuckled, and said, "Cynt, Dwight never left this facility. He was not in Panama City."

I could not believe what I had just heard! My mouth dropped wide open, and it took a few moments for me to shut it. I couldn't even form words to respond. I was just totally floored! You see, when Dwight called me on the day of the service and said that he was on 11th Street, I absolutely had no reason to believe that he was not. Dwight had pulled some stunts before, but this was the next level.

Charlie sort of laughed the whole thing off explaining that Dwight lives in his own world and his truth is his reality. He said that Dwight's pretending to be in Panama City to attend the service was his way of coping with Mama's passing and his version of closure. This was deep. I was used to dealing with my brothers' delusions, but this was mind-blowing.

When I spoke to Dwight, he never brought the situation up and neither did I. And to this day, he's never spoken about it.

That's just one example of what can happen when Dwight becomes delusional. I frequently encounter this when we talk, but never had I experienced it to that degree.

Frequently when we talk, Dwight is in the real world, but he can easily slip into becoming delusional. I'd love to be a fly on the walls of his mind to see what makes him tick. Of course, some of our best conversations are the ones where he is in the "real world," but they're often short lived. At any rate, it's a good feeling to know that my brother is still "in there."

Dwight and I spoke regularly after Mama passed, but things changed, and we didn't talk for a while. I was experiencing some rough patches in life and was preoccupied with my own drama.

One day Dwight felt heavy upon my mind, and I realized that it had been months since we'd spoken. I immediately picked up the phone to reach out to him. He was as happy to hear my voice as I was to hear his. We apologized to each other for not keeping in contact and ended up having a great conversation. After that, we started talking on a regular basis. Even though we never talked about it, I knew Dwight was still trying to come to grips with Mama's death. Mama had been Dwight's best friend.

We all knew how he felt about her, and of course, we knew how she felt about him. She was always there for him. Always. And now that she was gone, I could see that it was starting to take a toll on him.

I can't imagine what and how he must've been feeling. I couldn't have a conversation with him about Mama's death because when I had attempted to previously, it took him to a very dark place. A place that I knew he didn't need to be. So, I never said another word about Mama.

Delusional disorder is a type of mental health condition in which a person can't tell what's real from what's imagined. There are many types, including persecutory, jealous, and grandiose types. It's treatable with psychotherapy and medication.

(CLEVELAND CLINIC)

CHAPTER 22

MY BROTHER IS HUMAN

It's interesting how we can become so accustomed to the abnormal that we begin to accept it as normal.

It started to become increasingly difficult to understand Dwight during our phone calls. Then one day during one of our calls, it hit me like a ton of bricks. I noticed, as I had in times past, but had ignored it, that every time we would talk, he would be "out of it" for lack of a better way of putting it. When I say, "out of it," let me just describe what I mean. His speech would be so slurred that I could barely make out what he was saying. It would make for a difficult phone call because I would constantly have to ask him to repeat himself. I began hurrying to end our phone calls because it was simply too annoying to try to talk to him under those circumstances.

At other times, it would be Dwight who would become so frustrated to the point that he would just want to end the conversation. This went on for quite some time and I just sort of tolerated it as best I could. But the day that things hit me like a ton of bricks, was the day that I determined that some huge changes would need to take place in regard to my brothers' care. It suddenly dawned on me that my brother was leading a very poor quality of life. Yes, I understood that he was severely mentally ill and probably would be institutionalized for the rest of his life, but did that mean that he had to function like a zombie? That was exactly his case.

As Dwight and I talked that particular day and he started telling me how he felt, it was becoming more and more clear that some things needed to be addressed immediately. My heart was breaking into pieces as he was describing to me how he was feeling at that moment and how he felt the majority of the time.

We both knew it was the medication.

He said he felt sick, lethargic, and listless most of the time. He told me he didn't want to do anything. He said he couldn't even get out of bed most days for breakfast. He also told me that he couldn't even shave himself. As I sat there listening to all of this, more and more questions started running through my mind. One primary question was why did they have him on such a high dosage of medication to the point that he was unable to function?

As he continued describing how he felt, the wheels of my mind were spinning like crazy. The thought that came to mind was that the psychiatrists were just keeping him doped up because they didn't know what else to do with him. Before being permanently institutionalized, Dwight had always displayed very aggressive behavior, and now he was in a controlled environment where that could be monitored.

The fact that he was in a controlled environment certainly did not prevent his aggressive behavior; however, this just meant that now it could be more quickly brought under control. Since he was in a controlled environment, whenever he would become aggressive, I'm assuming that they would just increase the dosage of his medication to calm him down. The problem with that is, that became the norm, and it was the easiest way to fix the problem. The other problem was seemingly there was no happy medium with his medication dosage. Either he was practically nonfunctioning or bouncing off the walls. It seemed that barely functioning was the norm.

Enough was enough and it was time for me to intervene on behalf of my brother. I told Dwight to put his counselor on the phone so that I could speak with him.

When the counselor got on the phone and I expressed my concerns about how I believed my brother was being poorly treated, he became defensive. I will be the first to admit that I did not exercise much tact when confronting him, so I am not surprised that he became defensive. I told him that I felt that my brother was being treated inhumanely. I told him how I believed that there was no real thought being put into his care plan as far as medications were concerned. I told him that my brother was not an animal, but a human being and he deserved to be treated with some respect and dignity. I let him know that I loved my brother very much just in case there was a question about that. I demanded to know what meds he was on and how they were being administered, and also questioned him regarding team treatment meetings.

As I said, he became very defensive at first until I started using medical jargon that most laymen would not know. That's when he realized that he was not dealing with a novice in this area. He did an about-face and started giving me the answers to some probing questions that I had posed. Our conversation took a turn for the better and ended up being very productive. By the end of our conversation, I knew what meds my brother was taking, the dosage and how often those meds were being administered. For too long I had been somewhat lax in my involvement regarding my brothers' care, but those days were now behind me. I thought it was high time that I began watching my brother's progress more closely.

I decided that I needed to speak with Dwight at least once a week and that way I would be able to keep a close watch on how he was functioning.

Without giving Dwight full disclosure, I just suggested to him that I thought it would be a good thing if we started speaking at least once a week. He agreed and Dwight committed to speaking by phone weekly. The long overdue lengthy conversation with Dwight's counselor made all of the difference in the world. I was absolutely astounded at how Dwight's demeanor began to improve significantly within just a few short weeks. One of the things that Dwight's counselor and I had discussed during our conversation that day was that a new Medical Director was slated to come on board very soon. The counselor explained to me that, upon his arrival, the new psychiatrist intended to review each patient's current medication regimen and adjust it accordingly, if needed. I felt like he was just making this up to make things sound good, but later found that was not the case.

The new psychiatrist that had come on board had indeed taken a look at Dwight's medication regimen and adjusted it accordingly.

Within a few short weeks following his medication adjustments, when I would speak to Dwight on the phone, he was no longer sounding like somebody that was totally doped up. He was quite upbeat; not so upbeat that he was scaling the walls, but he sounded almost normal. Dwight told me that he felt so much better that he had started participating in extracurricular activities. I can't tell you how happy I was to know that my brother was getting the proper attention that he needed.

We kept our commitment to speak to each other at least once a week and things started getting better with Dwight from that point at least during that span of time. Dwight and I kept our weekly phone calls up for several weeks and then we started falling off the schedule. At first, we missed one week, then we missed two, then we missed three. And yes, you guessed it; before I knew it; we had gone a whole month without talking.

Although I knew this was happening and I knew where it was leading, I regretfully did not pull the reins on the situation before it got too far out of hand. One month turned into two and we were back to where we started before, we had made the agreement to talk once a week.

There were times when Dwight would call but my lifestyle had altered, and more often than not, I was not in a position to answer his calls. By the time I was able to return his call, it was too late because I was unable to contact him after a certain hour of the day. I could tell though that when Dwight would call me and leave a message, he just didn't sound right. Basically, his messages would be about me sending money. A few years prior, I offered to send Dwight money, but he refused stating that the state allowed him a certain amount of money each month and that if I sent him money as well that they would stop his stipend. He said he just preferred to receive money from the facility.

As time went on, he decided that yes, he did want me to send him money. He asked specifically for me to send him ten dollars a month, every third Wednesday. I agreed to do so but when the third Wednesday rolled around, I didn't send his money. I actually didn't get going with this until about two months later. By this time, Dwight had become upset with me and allowed it to be known through his counselor. CJ called me and said that he wanted to inform me that Dwight was upset with me because I was not sending money as promised. I asked CJ to please apologize to Dwight for me and to tell him that I would promptly send him money the following month. I did exactly what I said I would do, and all was well. But Dwight and I still had not spoken for some time. We eventually did speak, and I apologized to him for being late in sending him money. He accepted my apology, and all was well. I also mentioned that we had fallen off the schedule with our weekly calls and that we needed to get back on task. He agreed, but that never happened.

Time passed and we hadn't spoken for a good while when I received a call from Dwight, but I was not able to answer my phone when he called.

When I checked the message, he murmured something to me about sending him twenty dollars instead of ten dollars. I could tell from his speech that he not in a good space.

When I attempted to return Dwight's call, he would not accept my call. At that time, his counselor also informed me that Dwight was now depending on me to make sure that he had money. According to his counselor, for some reason, Dwight assumed that I had a lot of money. Nothing could have been further from the truth. It was no big deal that Dwight wanted me to send him money, after all, he was only asking for twenty dollars a month. That's not a lot of money, and I figured that the least that I could do for my brother was to honor that request.

I started sending him twenty dollars a month, although I will have to admit that I was not prompt in sending it on the third Wednesday of each month. I am making no excuses, but since I had to send the money in the form of a money order that was making things very difficult. One reason that it was difficult is that I very seldom carried cash on me and would go to purchase the money order without remembering to have cash on me. The stores accept cash only when you're purchasing a money order. So rather than leave the store and go to a nearby bank or ATM machine, and go back to purchase the money order, I would just go home and try it again the next day. Often times the next day would turn into the next day and the next day and before I realized it, several days would have passed before I had purchased the money order. What should have been the third Wednesday that the money order was sent to Dwight would often turn into one to two weeks later.

The more I thought about it, the more I believe my actions may have triggered Dwight negatively, and that's why he stopped wanting to talk to me. Not just my failure to send the money promptly, but also my negligence in consistently speaking with him once a week as we had decided. I regret that I didn't follow through because my brother shut me out and I didn't speak to him for a very long time.

Dwight and I eventually made contact again, but our phones calls are pretty much non-existent these days. The one consolation I have is at least the staff keeps me informed of my brothers' well-being, but I would love to hear his voice. I send him cards occasionally, but he never responds.

Dwight has been institutionalized for thirty-five years, and this will more than likely be his home until his dying day.

10 Ways to Support a Loved One in a Psychiatric Hospital:
- Use encouraging language.
- Make them laugh.
- Know your visiting options.
- Get creative.
- Play games.
- Bring them comfort items.
- Bring clothes.
- Use sensory items.
- Ask questions.
- Be forgiving.

(The Mighty)

CHAPTER 23

THINGS WEREN'T SUPPOSED TO HAPPEN THIS WAY

What are the chances that three of four siblings would be affected by a severe mental illness?

There is no way that my parents could have foreseen or imagined that three of their four beautiful children's lives would result in such a turn of dramatic events involving mental illness. I pity my Mama and Daddy who had to stand by helplessly so many times for many years and watch their three male children endure living in the dark shadows of mental illness for much of their lifetime. What had become of those bubbly bundles of joy that were supposed to end up being productive citizens of society? You know, those rising stars who someday would perhaps go to college and get their degree and become the next great lawyer or doctor. Or maybe even follow in Daddy's footsteps and become the best lawn care service in town. They would find that perfect mate to marry and together they would produce the next generation who would produce a legacy to be proud of.

As for me and my brothers, I'm sure that our idea of a happy life had included a set of loving and nurturing parents who would love and protect us from any harm at all costs. I'm not saying that we had to be the perfect family because I now know that doesn't exist.

Throughout the years, the two lingering questions that have been on my mind are: Why did it have to happen to my family, and how could things have played out differently? Over time I believe I've received some illumination surrounding these two questions.

The answer to the first question of why this happened to my family will never be known. However, being a woman of faith, I know that God in His sovereignty has His reasons.

What I do know is that I survived it all. For many years I have taken this for granted, but now I'm aware that my survival shouldn't be taken lightly. I could have easily suffered from mental illness as well. Not only that, but the destructive path that I would take from my late teens through my early twenties could have and should have taken me out. I'm sure a lot of what I chose to involve myself in during those reckless years was a direct result of what I had experienced around my brothers' mental health issues, although I didn't know that then. My life of promiscuity and experimenting with dangerous drugs was one that could have easily taken me out. But for the grace of God, I made it through those tumultuous times.

The second question of how things could have played out differently has certainly been answered.

I am convinced that had there been EARLY INTERVENTION during the onset of my brothers' mental health issues, they would have had a better chance of managing their illnesses.

I believe that the lack of early intervention impeded my brothers' abilities to successfully manage their illnesses, and their stories ended tragically. I continue to mourn their chance to live ordinary, productive, and fulfilling lives.

A complex mental illness inevitably impacts everyone in the family. Siblings indirectly affected by their brother or sister's severe mental illness may experience a complicated range of emotions, many of which are disturbing and stressful and may require extra effort to overcome. While parental support can be helpful, individual, and family counseling may be needed in these situations to help siblings cope with their own mental health challenges.

(BRIGHTQUEST TREATMENT CENTERS)

CHAPTER 24

MY STORY—PART I

I know you're wondering how I survived it all—why crazy didn't get ME!

This was probably the hardest chapter of the book for me to write. I had to dig way down to answer that question.

I alluded earlier to some of my risky behaviors that more than likely were brought on by all of the drama and trauma of living with siblings who were ALL mentally ill, but let me share some details.

Well, the long and short answer is, BUT God. At the end of the day, I know that it was absolutely NOBODY but God! Why He would choose me to be the one to "make it out," I'll never know.

Science may have an explanation for the mental illness in my family involving genes and chromosomes, DNA, and the likes, since only the males were affected. I don't believe it had anything to do with science. Trust me, anyone having to deal with what I dealt with growing up in THAT house more than likely would not have escaped a mental illness.

At times, during casual conversation about my book, I will jokingly say crazy didn't get me, but if you push me too far, you might just see a little crazy.

On a more serious note, as I reflect back as far as I can remember, I have always been strong, a fighter, and resilient. I'm kind of ashamed to admit it, but many times I have had a habit of burying my head in the sand and not acknowledging what was going on around me, especially if it was negative. Now that could be good or bad. What I believe about myself is that it was definitely a survival tool. You see, when I just pretended the problem wasn't there, I wasn't fazed by what was happening around me. I figured that things would eventually take care of themselves.

As am writing this, I'm reminded of how I felt "different" from my friends because they always seemed to have a sibling around to stick up for them if they ever got in trouble, especially in school.

The problem for me was since there was a five-year gap between me and my youngest brother, each time I was entering my next school, he was leaving. It bothered me that I didn't have a sibling at my school like most of my friends.

I know I suffered from low self-esteem because most of my friends had "nice" homes and ours wasn't the best. Not only that, but I was also often teased about my big forehead, my gap, and my dark skin. Unfortunately, to make matters worse, my Mama never validated me. She never let me forget that I was "dark-skinned" and had a "big forehead."

I was never a part of the clique. Back then, I'd say I was the odd girl out. I still am truth be told. Not only that, but I also always talked extremely loud. I remember one day when I was visiting my friend's house, I overheard her older sister say, "I don't want that Mobley girl over here because she talks too loud." That hurt.

I can recall being bullied by one of my classmates almost every day as we walked home from school. She never hit me, but she verbally taunted me.

It didn't help that we didn't have a T.V. at home and everyone knew it. I recall getting into a fight with one of my classmates after school one day because she was going around saying we didn't have a T.V. because my Mama was "too saved." Well, the truth is she was telling the TRUTH!

It's becoming clearer now how early on many of my experiences were toughening me up for what I would eventually have to endure with my brothers' mental health issues. I was learning how to take a licking and keep on ticking. If I could borrow a famous line from The Color Purple, "All my life I had to fight."

One of a few great memories that I have of my grade school years is when my Mama MADE me memorize the names of the sixty-six books of the Bible. I'd always been great at memorizing stuff, and Mama would put that to use. Once she knew that I was able to run right through those sixty-six books without missing a beat, she put me up in front of our local church to recite them. From that time on, whenever there was any type of program at church, I would be placed on the program to recite the names of the sixty-six books of the Bible. I suppose that boosted my self-esteem quite a bit because after all, nobody else could do that. It was bitter-sweet though because during Vacation Bible School, I ticked everyone off when we would play the game of seeing who could find a scripture the fastest. Since I knew the order of the books in the bible, I always won.

Fast forward to my middle school years and the first thing that comes to mind is that of me being a tomboy. I wasn't very concerned about how I looked or what I wore. I was convinced that I was ugly because I was dark-skinned with a gap and a big forehead. They didn't say much about my complexion and my gap during middle school, but I was reminded daily about my big forehead. I was called names like, bus forehead, triple deck, and shiny ball. A day didn't pass that I wasn't called at least one of those names if not all of them. All I can say is kids can be cruel. Funny thing is I never hated them for what they said to me, I just often wondered how they could be so mean. I couldn't help how God made me. I never retaliated because I was too afraid. After all, I didn't have a sibling to stand up for me. Rather than buckle under the pressure, this made me tougher than nails.

Since I didn't care much for my appearance and was a tomboy; my best friend got all the boyfriends. She was "light-skinned" and considered "pretty." The boys never took a second look at me. I knew they didn't think I was pretty and that hurt, but I dealt with it. Boy, if they could see me now!

I managed to get through middle school despite the constant teasing and rejection.

And then came my high school years. My sophomore year was pretty uneventful. I got along well with everyone, but I must have had a way with words. I remember my English teacher saying to me one day, "Cynthia, don't speak so harshly." I'm sorry she felt that way, but I guess life up to this point had made me a bit hardened. I also remember being a kick-butt typist because I nailed every typing test. My fingers just flew across that keyboard. I not only typed fast but with accuracy.

A fond memory of being in tenth grade was of my Public Speaking teacher. She was very funny. When we were asked to introduce ourselves on the first day of class, I said my name was Cynthia, but they called me Cynt. She thought I said Cyn, so she always teased me and called me "Sin."

I don't remember much about my junior year except that I had a summer job between my junior and senior years. I worked as a clerk-typist at the Civil Engineering Center at Tyndall Air Force Base.

By this time, I was no longer a tomboy. I looked pretty good, and a few of the enlisted guys noticed. So much so that one guy tried to corner me in the conference room one day at work. We played cat and mouse around that room until I was able to maneuver to the door and escaped his clutches. I can only imagine what he planned to do to me if he had caught me.

I also had to jump from a moving car one day when I was offered a ride home from work with someone whom I trusted. I guess my Mama never told me not to get in cars with strangers. I worked in the same office with this guy who was a sergeant and appeared to be very mild-mannered. Everything was going fine until he passed the street where I told him I lived. When I told him so, he ignored me. I knew that something was wrong, and this was not going to turn out good for me. All I know is when he slowed down to make a turn; I opened the door and jumped out of the moving car.

Imagine having to face the guy at work who was trying to corner me in the conference room and this guy from whose car I had to jump. I didn't tell anyone because I thought no one would believe me. Afterall, who would believe a sixteen-year-old clerk-typist over these airmen? Well, maybe they would have believed me. At any rate, I just kept things to myself and steered clear of both of those monsters.

I made it through the summer, and it was time for my senior year of high school. In nine months, I would finally be able to sing, "Schools' out for summer, schools' out Forever!"

I remember spending all of my paychecks that I'd made that summer on school clothes. Like my Mama, I had fashion sense and expensive taste, so I went to school my senior year dressed to the nines.

One day I was in the bathroom, inside the stall, when I heard two girls come in and they were having a conversation, and the conversation happened to be about yours truly. To this day, I will never forget what the one girl said in reference to me. She said, "I hate her." Little did they know who was in the stall. I remained there until they left the bathroom because I didn't want them to know that I had heard what they'd said about me.

CHAPTER 25

MY STORY—PART II

My senior year proved to be quite interesting to say the least. I didn't have a second or third period, and my friend Missy and I would always ride off campus. She was from a wealthy family and owned a car. A Ford Mustang to be exact. We would always go to McDonalds or some other restaurant and get food. I remember that we were the first people to sample Captain D's food. It was a new restaurant that was opening in Panama City, and Missy knew the owners. The day that we decided to stop by the restaurant was prior to opening and the owners wanted guinea pigs to test out the food. We'll they'd found two. I must say that the food was extremely delicious.

Missy and I would also often visit their new home that was being built. My, what a beautiful home it was! Missy's father was a doctor and they had money. I will never forget that there was a huge tree on the property and rather than cut the tree down, a certain part of the home was built around the tree. That was one of the most amazing sights I've ever seen.

As my senior year moved along, I started to become involved in certain activities. For kicks and giggles, I ran for president of the Future Business Leaders of America and much to my surprise, I won. I didn't have a clue as to what I was supposed to be doing. I joined the Civic Club, just because, and the Concert Choir. And last but not least, I ran for Homecoming Queen, and was a Miss Valentine's Day Contestant. I didn't place in either and I didn't care. I was doing stuff just to be doing stuff. Running for Homecoming Queen did get me a spot in the local newspaper and my Mama was as proud as a peacock.

Those were the good memories of my senior year. But there were a few bad ones as well.

My worst memory of my senior year was that of being bullied. Two girls were jealous of my friend and me and decided to bully us after school every day as we walked home. My friend and I were "church girls," so we weren't accustomed to fighting. Those two girls were thuggish and apparently lacked home training. I say this because when we told my friend's mama what was going on, she confronted one of the girls mamas and to my knowledge the lady didn't think it was a big deal and sort of condoned her daughters' actions. I didn't bother to tell my Mama because I already knew she wouldn't do anything. So, my friend and I continued to be bullied until one day we got fed up. My friend decided to take a knife to school one day and stab the girls when they started taunting us after school. Like clockwork, as we began our walk home, the bullies showed up. Little did they know my friend had a knife. As one girl was walking very close to my friend while taunting her, my friend murmured under her breath to me that she was about to stab the girl. She had rolled the knife up in a sweater with the tip pointed toward the other girl's side. Mind you, she had sharpened the blade to the point where you could barely touch it without being cut. As my friend continued to murmur to me that she was about to stab the other girl, I started begging my friend not to do it.

The foolish girl had no clue that she was a hair away from getting stabbed. As sharp as that knife was, she would've probably bled out and died before she could get medical attention.

About that time, my cousin pulled up in his car, and sensing there was a problem, he told us to get in the car. My friend got in my cousin's car, but I refused. I was sick and tired of these bullies, and I wasn't going to be frightened away by them.

Well, I was left alone with these two thugs and still had at least a mile and a half to go before I would be near my house.

Of course, they continued to taunt me. I'd finally had enough and thought this needed to be settled once and for all. I flung off my coat and challenged one of the girls to a fight. I got up in her face and told her to come on, let's go at it. Much to my surprise, she sheepishly backed away and didn't respond to my challenge.

As we neared the corner store where some of the older guys would hang out, someone yelled out to the bully that I'd challenged earlier that her brother was there. Before I knew what was happening, she had grabbed me from behind and we started wrestling. Mind you, this girl had a solid build, and was much taller and bigger than me. We finally wrestled each other to the ground. I was wearing a dress that day, and as we rolled around on the ground, I noticed one of the guys positioning himself to look under my dress. When I saw that, I immediately stopped wrestling, crossed my legs, and laid still.

I can't believe what happened next. That girl savagely sank her teeth into one of my jaws and held on for a moment. She finally let go and we stopped wrestling. I got up from the ground and for some reason, she left me alone. I bore her teeth marks on my jaw for quite some time. Every time I looked at my face, I was reminded of that horrible experience. But can I tell you that after that day, those girls never bothered us again. I guess all it took was finally standing up for myself. Even though it appeared that I lost that fight, as far as I'm concerned, I won. I won because I stood up for myself, which was more than I had done before.

I mentioned before that I was involved in several extracurricular activities during my senior year, however; there was one particular activity that I was involved in that no one was aware of, and it had nothing to do with school. I met a boy that I liked. He had already graduated from high school but would often hang out across the street from the school as many of the guys did. It wasn't long before we started seeing each other and I began sneaking out of class to spend time with him. I would literally climb out of my classroom window when the teacher wasn't watching. Little did I know that my little extracurricular activities would eventually change the trajectory of my life.

As I was nearing the end of my senior year, it seemed like I was becoming more and more adventurous. I remember coming home from school one day and not being in a very good mood. That was the day that my youngest brother introduced me to marijuana. I was telling him that I was feeling down and out, and his response to me was, "you wanna smoke a joint?" I was somewhat taken aback, but I said yes, and pot became my new favorite thing to do. When I would smoke, I could temporarily escape all of my problems. But we know that once the high wore off, I was still facing those same problems.

Well, I survived the remainder of my senior year and graduated in 1977. I was free at last, free at last! I didn't have to worry about school anymore, thank God. I never liked it anyway. Now I could smoke pot as often as I pleased and just live my life foot-loose and fancy free. My parents kept bugging me about college, so finally sixth months after graduating from high school, I enrolled in community college to get them off my back. I was taking evening classes. One advantage to this was I was allowed to drive Daddy's car to class.

My three older brothers had never been allowed to drive Daddy's car, so this was a privilege. I went to class for one semester and quit, although my parents weren't aware. I would leave home as if I were headed to class, but instead went to hang out with my friends. On Wednesday evenings, I would go to the club and party. Funny, my parents never asked me about my grades, and of course, I never mentioned it. Well, there was nothing to mention. To this day, I don't know if they were on to me or not. If they were, they never said anything. After some time, I guess it didn't really matter. I had become that girl that lived to smoke pot and party. I mentioned earlier that three months after graduating from high school, I discovered I was pregnant. Sad but true, that didn't stop me from getting high and partying. What was I thinking? I was living the life, or so I thought.

CHAPTER 26

MY STORY—PART III

I was eighteen years old when I gave birth to my son on November 26th, 1977. I thank God that despite the fact that I smoked marijuana practically every day while I was pregnant, I delivered a healthy 6 lbs., 1.5 oz. baby boy. I would love to say that having the responsibility of caring for another human being matured me and caused me to change some of my bad habits, but it didn't, not one bit. I continued getting high and partying. Since I still lived at home, most of the time I would either sneak out or just walk out the door and leave my parents and or my brother to babysit my son. I didn't care, I was living for the party. I was clearly on a mission to destroy my life.

Some of the worst years in my adult life were between the ages of nineteen and twenty-two. I was nineteen when Daddy died and after his death, I didn't really care about much. Talking about being on a mission to destroy my life, it got real.

One day I said to my Mama that I was going to be like my Daddy. I was going to do everything that I was big enough to do, and then give my life to the Lord. Mama's response was simply, "You might not make it."

Well, I took my quest for self-destruction to a new level. I was out of control. Marijuana had taken over my life and I did whatever it took to get my hands on it. I ended up pawning my class ring and the typewriter Mama bought me as a gift for my high school graduation.

I once bought weed with the money that Mama gave me to pay our electric bill, and our lights were turned off. In addition, I wrote worthless checks at grocery stores to get cash back to support my habit. The worst thing I did was buy weed with the money that was designated for my baby's pampers. I was rapidly sinking into an abyss that I could not seem to pull myself from. Believe it or not, despite all of this, I somehow managed to keep a job.

One day I was arrested for writing the bad checks but was released on my own recognizance. I don't recall ever appearing in court to face those charges. I kept writing the bad checks, but not facing the music and somehow just kept slipping through the cracks.

But one day, my criminal and destructive behavior caught up to me, and that's when I was arrested and landed in jail for fourteen days with no bond. I guess neither my Mama nor my supervisor at work understood the words, no bond because as hard as they tried to get me released, it was not happening. I would spend fourteen days in jail. That had to be one of the worst experiences I'd ever had in my life. I vowed to God and myself that once I got out of jail that I would turn my life around, specifically stop smoking marijuana. Boy, it's amazing the promises you'll make when you're in crisis mode. The day finally came for my release from jail and the first thing I did was go looking for some weed. Apparently, I hadn't yet learned my lesson.

But this time around, the stint was short. My life was about to take a turn for the better. I was out with my niece one evening, high as a kite. As usual I was settling in for a long night of partying when I remembered that I had promised someone that I would attend church with him that evening. I abruptly said to my niece to take me home. Normally, she would have said to me that she would take me home when she was ready. But this time, she didn't say that. She took me home, I showered and by the time my friend came to pick me up for church, I was no longer high.

Something happened to me that night in 1985, and my life of getting high, partying, and sexual promiscuity was about to become a thing of the past. I accepted Jesus into my life, and the rest was history. I kept to the narrow path.

I met and married my first husband who was also a Christian and a minister. I ended up accepting my call to the ministry in 1985 and was subsequently licensed and ordained. Unfortunately, that marriage ended after five years due to infidelity on his part.

Approximately two years later, I met and married my second husband, and was married to him around two years before that marriage ended. He was physically abusive.

That second marriage drove me away from my hometown of Panama City, Florida in 1996 to Pittsburgh, Pennsylvania. I was there for six years when I met my third husband. We are currently separated but remain friends. He's a great guy.

The separation from my third husband took me back to my hometown of Panama City, Florida in December 2017. I was there for ten months when Hurricane Michael hit and devastated Panama City. The place where I was living was pretty much destroyed, and I was forced to relocate yet again in October of 2018 to Central Florida. My move to Central Florida has proven to be one of the best things that has ever happened in my life.

I give thanks to God first, then to my beautiful cousin who so graciously opened the doors of her beautiful home to me. I've been blessed to have been planted in a wonderful church where I am fully thriving.

The trajectory of my life was altered once again in 2020 with the outbreak of COVID-19. Just as Hurricane Michael could have been devastating for me, but instead it proved to be a good thing, so it was with COVID -19 as well. The pandemic was an opportunity for me to evaluate my life in a deeper way. I decided during that time that life was fleeting. It was time for me to take the brakes off and step out into my entrepreneurial journey and everything else that I'd been snoozing on.

In 2021, I co-authored my first book which was an Amazon #1 Best Seller. I founded my business, HoWELL ARE YOU, which is a health and wellness business registered in the State of Florida. In addition, I was chosen to speak at the Leadership Experience Tour, which is the #1 platform in the US for aspiring speakers. The event was held at the Embassy Suites in Troy, Michigan, and I gave a moving rendition of what it was like growing up in a house where ALL of my siblings were affected by a severe mental illness.

Since that time, I have become known as the mental health advocate whose mantra is, "I'm Not Keeping Quiet Anymore." I even started a t-shirt line that says that. Since that time, I've become an International Speaker and frequent talk show/podcast guest, where I continue to share my story about sibling mental illness, with a focus on early intervention.

And last but certainly not least, after struggling to lose unwanted pounds for several years, I began a plant food lifestyle in 2019. Since that time, I've lost more than forty pounds, and have leveled up to a raw vegan diet. I'm a Certified Transformational Coach and have designed a coaching program to help others make the transition to a plant food lifestyle. These are just a few of my many accomplishments.

Although it looked as if the odds were stacked against me, I defied the odds. I overcame bullying, but most of all, I overcame the stigma of being raised in a home where they said we were ALL CRAZY! No, crazy DID NOT GET ME!

EPILOGUE

I always say that my family paid the supreme price for keeping quiet about my brothers' mental health issues. And that's precisely why I'm committed to advocating for the mentally ill. One of the ways that I advocate is by keeping the conversation going. Remember, my mantra is, "I'm Not Keeping Quiet Anymore," and I'm NOT! I will continue to raise the awareness regarding mental illness until there is not a single breath left in my body! I will NOT be silenced!

At the completion of this manuscript, we've discovered that my brother, Donny who has been missing for over two decades, is alive. It's been verified through the Social Security administration that Donny is receiving benefits, but listed as homeless. Therefore, we still don't know where he is. My brother Dwight is still institutionalized and hasn't wanted to speak with me for several months now. Sadly, Dwight will probably be institutionalized until his dying day, but at least I know where he is.

I hope that by being fully transparent about my family's experience surrounding sibling mental illness, other families can see that they are not alone and the sooner they can get professional treatment for their loved one, the better.

I encourage those who are in the faith-based community to come alongside the mental health community and help to raise awareness. In addition, I encourage those affected with a mental illness to combine professional treatment and prayer. If you could PRAY mental illness away, you wouldn't be reading this book right now.

I want to stress that there is NO SHAME in asking for help. Ultimately, if I can prevent just one family from experiencing the pain that mine did, I would consider that a success.

Now, I know why **CRAZY DIDN'T GET ME**! What I went through and overcame was **PREPARATION FOR MY DESTINY**.

The Beginning . . .

ACKNOWLEDGMENTS

First and FOREMOST, to my Father God who is the ultimate inspiration for me writing this book and who has made me to know that with Him, ALL things are possible!

To my Daddy and Mama; Oliver Sr., and Florence Ruby Pittman Mobley, who brought me up in the nurture and the admonition of the Lord, and who did the best they could in parenting; may you continue to rest in peace.

To my three 'whys,' James, Billy (Donny), and Dwight, may God hold you in his loving arms and give you peace. To my dear son Marcus, whom I love and cherish deeply.

Ray, who is ALWAYS just a phone call away, my childhood friend, Lizzette, who ALWAYS believed in me, my sister from another mother, Beverly Lynn a constant source of support in SO MANY WAYS, my long-time friend/brother; Evangelist Wesley 'Panama' Watkins, Jr. for your wise counsel, and to my childhood classmate and long-time friend Gregory S. Dossie, for ALWAYS supporting my mission. To all of these amazing people, I owe you a debt of gratitude.

To these special people who ALL helped to make this book a reality; I offer my sincere heartfelt appreciation:

Brenda Moton, Gladys Davis Daniels, Harry and La-Nita Boston, Jasmine Allen, Kevin and Linda Curry, Apostle Lee Lyons, Ruby Allen, Reverend David McWilliams, Rhonda Jones, Dr. Sherry Taylor-Butler, Tiffany Render, Reverend and Minister Tyrone and Joanne Jordan, and Pastor Darryl Church and First Lady Valencia.

And last but certainly not least, thank you to my Editor, Melanie James and Designer, Juan Roberts.

ABOUT THE AUTHOR

Cynthia Mobley Howell is a lifestyle transformer, minister, and plant-based wellness advocate who embodies the power of intentional reinvention. A self-described late bloomer, Cynthia began her transformative journey later in life-releasing over 70 pounds while gaining something even greater: clarity, courage, and alignment.

This relaunch reflects not a rewrite of her story, but a refinement of it. Grounded in faith and lived experience, Cynthia's work centers on whole-person wellness-spirit, soul, and body-and the belief that growth does not expire. Her voice speaks to women who know there is more ahead and are ready to step into it with wisdom, confidence, and purpose.

Cynthia's message is simple yet bold: new beginnings are not reserved for the young-they are claimed by the willing.

www.ingramcontent.com/pod-product-compliance
Lightning Source LLC
Chambersburg PA
CBHW051518120626
46551CB00012B/982